27 Seconds

The Revolutionary Look
Into the Culture of
Domestic Sex Trafficking

Anny Donewald & Joshua Robison

Printed in the United States of America

First Printing, 2018

ISBN 978-0-692-07900-3

**A portion of the proceeds from the sale of "27 Seconds" goes to
Eve's Angels and The Armed Campaign.
For more information, go to:**

www.evesangels.org

www.armedcampaign.org

THE FIGHT SONG....

In the summer of 2016 there was a sequence of events that happened in a very short period of time which required an intense amount of focus. The goal was to raise, in twelve weeks, the full amount for Eve's Angels' safe home, ensuring no financial overhang payments or any circumstance that would ever cause us to lose it. With Eve's Angels' past and present financial ceiling 1/10, of what the need was to accomplish the goal, the task was going to require a miracle.

As I sat completely overwhelmed with what was required and the impossibility that stood between me and all of the women my heart bled for, I prayed real simple: "God.... there is absolutely no way I can do this. But You can. I'm gonna give this everything I got. But the increase is up to You. If it doesn't work, I'll take it as a sign that it's time to dissolve the organization and I'm done with this part of my life. But I'm going to give this everything I have so I never look back and wonder, 'What if I would've tried this'........ok Jesus.... Show me the way."
That one prayer sealed my fate.

The first two weeks were spent on strategizing--the "how do you eat an elephant" sort of thing where I was getting organized, figuring out grant writing, online marketing, newsletters etc.; I had to figure out a "flow". I spoke briefly to a close friend of mine from high school who'd called to check on me. At the time, he was dating a single mother whose son he'd spend time with--the little boy's father wasn't active in his life. My friend noticed a lack of discipline and a tendency to pull on his mother's "heart strings" by becoming overly emotional in an attempt to get his mother to do what he wanted. My friend went on to tell me how he'd spent time at their house, and when it was time to pick up his toys, so they could get ready to go to the park, the child tried to do the same thing with my friend as he'd done with his mom. My friend, (genius as always) stepped in

2

during the little boy's meltdown and said, "Ok little buddy--here's the deal. I'm not going to tell you NOT to cry. I'm not going to tell you how to feel at all. I'm going to stop what we're doing and give you 30 seconds to cry and get everything out. I'm going to time you. OK? So, when you start crying, cry with everything in you. You can yell, and snot, and scream, and make the ugly cry face and wail as loud as you need to. But when the 30 seconds is up, we have to finish what we were doing." As the story went, my friend started the timer, and as he counted down the last few seconds, the little boy wiped his face and stopped crying at 28 seconds and, with a huge smile on his face said, "THERE! I DID IT!!!"

As days and weeks passed during my push to secure the funding for the safe home, there were times where I'd get so overwhelmed with what was at stake, how much further I had to go, how exhausted I was, etc., that I started to doubt my ability to pull it off. About 3-4 weeks of working and working and working and barely any results, I broke down and started to cry. My first thought was, "I don't have time for this!!!" And then I heard my friend's voice say, "Ok little buddy--here's the deal. I'm not going to tell you NOT to cry. I'm not going to tell you how to feel at all. I'm going to stop what we're doing and give you 30 seconds to cry and get everything out. I'm going to time you. OK? So, when you start crying, cry with everything in you. You can yell, and snot, and scream, and make the ugly cry face and wail as loud as you need to. But when the 30 seconds is up, we have to finish what we were doing."

My next thought was, "Well if a child can do it in 28 seconds, I got this in 27. I'm going to time it because while I'm crying about being overwhelmed with what I perceive is a problem, someone just like me is being sold for sex, and if they try to escape for their life, they're going to need a safe place to go. They need me to finish this."

And as the story went, any time I'd get that feeling where I was about to break from the reality of what I was attempting to do and the urgency of it, and the flashbacks and the desperation of not being crushed under the kind of pressure that sits on you when you know lives are at stake, and you know you have little time to make sure you can hide them when they're running......I'd set the timer for 27 seconds.

When you understand the depth and darkness of sex trafficking and the strength it takes to endure life during (and after), it reminds you that your problems are a matter of perspective. When you've been a product to be sold in the underworld, you grow callous to mainstream cultural problems when someone goes into a fit of rage and their day is ruined because the barista forgot to use soy milk. When you've been there, you understand the urgency to help people that are trapped in a level of darkness few have seen, and most can't describe. I carried it. I carried it the entire 12 weeks (and what I realized later-in a way I wasn't even aware of- I carried it my entire life). I fought with everything in me for women I'd met, women I knew, women I would meet--the woman I'd been, the woman I was, the woman I am, and I will always be. I AM her. And I fought for her, and for all of us because, what if I could make a difference. What if I get this done. The inspiration, the tenacity, the focus, the grit and the very pressure of knowing how horrible that life is firsthand was the fuel to reach the finish-line. Freedom was my end goal.

Within the pages of this book contain the unveiling of a world you most likely know nothing about. It is a gift from me to you -- an inside look into what sex trafficking is, how it works, why it is, what it is etc. As you take it in, there are going to be times where you're going to want to set this book down and pretend as if you don't know -- that you don't see. You'll want to put your rose-colored glasses back on and go complain about how the barista forgot to use the soy milk. I'm challenging you that, when that happens, put the book down. Set a timer for 27 seconds. And hear me say, "OK little buddy--here's the deal. I'm not going to tell you NOT to cry. I'm not going to tell you how to feel at all. I'm going to stop what we're doing and give you 27 seconds to cry and get everything out.

I'm going to time you. OK? So, when you start crying, cry with everything in you. You can yell, and snot, and scream, and make the ugly cry face and wail as loud as you need to. But when the 27 seconds is up, we have to finish what we were doing."

The Starting Lineup

THE PREVIOUS PLAYBOOK

I. The Previous Playbook

Deconstructing Previous and Current Research and Data: Why the Content

Dr. Suzie Sunshine is a major public health figure. She is a researcher who carries two PhDs. She got her Doctorate of Public Health through the University of Michigan in which she graduated summa cum laude. After witnessing the atrocities that women face within our Public Health Sector, she decided to go back to school and get her PhD in Social Work from Michigan State University. She is now known as the leading researcher and expert in the country. She applies her thorough research techniques to an uncharted subject: misunderstood and marginalized groups of people. Because of the respect and trust she has garnered, she now has access to the different knowledge bases that these groups hold. As a trained social worker, she is able to create infrastructures within her private practice to help these marginalized groups. In addition to creating specific infrastructures to help these groups, her aptitude as a researcher has allowed her to collect a large volume of empirical data. With her educational background, success in her private practice and aptitude for research, many people believe that she will be the leading expert in understanding women who belong to a newly identified group: trafficked victims from the Sex for Sale epidemic.

There is a tremendous disconnect between the length of time that victims and survivors of trafficking have been identified as a people group to be studied, versus the length of time that the sex-for-sale subculture has actually existed. This disconnect puts any researcher at such a massive disadvantage that their research is set up to fail. Why is this? The reason is simple: anyone from outside the sex-for-sale subculture has deep unconscious conditioning. It is this conditioning that creates the false data and reporting.

False data is a fundamental and widespread problem. It is partially a result of society's unconscious conditioning, and also from the well-intentioned mass educational push to provide "awareness and services" for women who need it. "Sex trafficking" has become a new buzz word in the last decade, and without the proper tools to understand the system and how it works, we are making the problem worse. Furthermore, we are ill-equipped to serve the victims and survivors.

Currently, only a survivor of this crime is the expert, but only to the point at which she's healed can she lend her expertise. Survivors have faced their traumas and relive them each time they educate and advocate. The lack of understanding into the sex for sale epidemic by the general public has created an isolation factor where each survivor is not only left to understand and process, but is simultaneously interpreting and educating the general public. Unfortunately, because "trafficking" is the new cultural buzz word, not everyone who speaks is an expert, and not every expert is a true survivor. Due to this internal journey each victim must take to become a survivor, in as much as she's dug deep and made peace with the personal injustice done to her can she surface back up with priceless treasures that then qualify her to be an expert. No other research is accurate; there hasn't been enough understanding and time to set up measurable data on what trafficking is, who it affects, who it targets, how it works and what it looks like.

The idea that someone could understand women from a culture that has had centuries of stereotyped lies is the fallacy that has led to the enduring misconceptions that these women face. Furthermore, the fact that trafficking continues to rise as the largest and fastest-growing form of criminal activity proves that slavery is not something of the past. This is where Doctor Sunshine's research has failed.[1]

To understand requires a person who speaks the language of the subculture; she is able to interpret the ways in which the system works, how it is set up, and who is involved. Albert Einstein said it best, "We cannot solve problems by using the same kind of thinking we used when we created them."[2] In order to solve the problem, we have to understand what created it to begin with.

Mainstream society's conditioned biases toward sex workers creates a blind spot; this blind spot results in inaccurate data. Researchers are trying to collect data from the outside looking in, taking subjects and turning women in this industry into scientific lab rats, racing to find the key as to why this population exists. However, due to the lack of knowledge from the people reporting and the measures being used, what they are looking at is foreign since their measures being used are interpreted through "dirty lenses." Their translation of the information is therefore, incorrect. In the commercial sex industry, words mean different things, time serves different purposes, love and rape are programmatically reversed and the intentions of control and lust for power creates the illusion that women's sexuality is for sale and money is worth a human life.

There is a negative stigma placed on sex-workers in the United States. Due to this stigma, biases exist in the mainstream subconscious. It is important as professionals to acknowledge any personal biases toward the women within this industry. Many professionals such as Dr. Sunshine certainly cannot understand why people may join the sex industry and continue to stay there. These professionals seek to answer the question, "Why?" for themselves, rather than asking the true expert, "Why?" Moreover, to further understand and effectively be able to assist in the healing of this minority group, it is essential to focus on the subculture as a whole and how this culture was created to begin with. Through awareness, education, understanding, and compassion, we then can work together to take the necessary steps to abolish this insidious crime of slavery.

If we liken this to learning about another country, we better understand the most effective mechanisms to reach our end goal: the abolishment of objectifying and selling people. This doesn't come by studying it in a textbook or an article reported by Dr. Sunshine. An unknown culture needs to be understood in its totality with interpretation of its moving parts including the nuances, laws, and rules of engagement. Each moving part plays a major role in comprehending the totality of the whole. While a traditional classroom environment will provide you with the technical communicative tools such as diction and grammar, the best way to fully understand a culture (especially for those who are trying to report accurate data) is best accomplished only when a full working knowledge of the culture and all of its components are understood. The sum total must be internally integrated into the psyche of the "outsider." Until then, a translator is needed from the subculture itself thereby identifying and instructing which tools are what and how to use each tool.

As professionals, we cannot put ourselves in the shoes of the people we are trying to help if we have never experienced the culture ourselves. We lack the understanding of what it is we're looking at. Furthermore, professionals can never put themselves in the shoes of the people within this industry. This means that we can only formulate a logical conception of what our client may be going through based on our own experiences and the things we've been socially programmed to believe about women who've sold sex. To formulate a better understanding of people within the sex industry, we must rid ourselves of any implicit bias that we may have. Above all, we must try to understand this culture from the perspective of those within the sex industry—and think of those people not as objects, but as your grandmother, your beloved mother, your sister, or your baby girl.

When No Means Yes

2. WHEN NO MEANS YES

SUGAR VS. SHARON

Once-upon-a-time there was a princess named Sugar. Sugar grew up in a middle-class family. Her parents got divorced when she was five, and although she saw her dad on Wednesday nights and every other weekend, her mother had a boyfriend that watched her after school for a few hours when Sugar's mom was working.

What Sugar's parents didn't know was that mom's boyfriend was sexually violating Sugar and threatening that she'd never see her dad again if she told. Finally, when Sugar was eleven, her mother broke up with the boyfriend because she found violent pornography once again on his computer. Sugar kept his secret and just… "moved on."

When Sugar got older, she dropped out of school. In an attempt to not add financial stress to her already struggling single mother, she worked as a waitress at the local strip club. Soon, she decided that dancing wasn't "that bad," and took her place sliding down the "rabbit pole." The strip club she worked at had a policy called "buyout." The customer would pay $500 to the club to get a girl of his choice to leave her shift early—essentially buying her out of her shift—and take her either to a hotel or to his house to engage in sex for sale. One night, Sugar was "bought out" and proceeded to go with her customer to his house. Upon entering the home, she was gang raped by him and several of his roommates. Sugar was set up, and no money was exchanged. In any other world, this would be larceny. But not in Sugar's world. Let's explore why.

Someone recently asked me if Princess Sugar went to the hospital after her trauma and got a rape kit and if she'd filed a police report. After I picked my jaw up off the floor at the ignorance of the question, I walked them through the absurdity of their question. Here's why a police report doesn't work in this culture: Let's say Sugar, after being raped by five men on an escorting call, left the crime scene and went to the police station. Here's how that sounds:

Sugar: Hi. I need to file a police report. I've just been violently gang raped and robbed on a work call.

Police: OK. (takes out pen and paper). Where were you and who was it that did this felonious crime? Was it a stranger? A friend? Were you on a date?

Sugar: Well, I was at work at the strip club, a client came in and paid the buyout amount to the club and hired me for sex. I went to his house and instead of the mutual exchange of selling sex for money, I was gang raped by him and four of his roommates instead. He stole from me; I never received the money he owed me. Only the club did.

Police: You have the right to remain silent. Everything you say can and will be used against you in a court of law.

Note to the reader: If the **ONLY** response from law enforcement is the Miranda warning and immediate arrest for prostitution, she got lucky. Women from the sex trade know that when a police officer is informed of our places of employment, we're at high risk for further rape and assault by those that swear to protect and serve. Furthermore, in some states, it's legal to rape a sex worker taken into custody.[3] The cultural viewpoint as a whole is that you can't rape a hooker. Clearly, we asked for it.

LET'S NOW TAKE A LOOK AT A WOMAN NAMED SHARON

Sharon grew up in a middle-class family. Her parents divorced, and her mom remarried a great guy named Bruce. Upon completing high school, Sharon finds out she's pregnant with her boyfriend Bill's love child. Bill "does the right thing" and marries Sharon. Bill goes on to college with the help of his family and obtains a college degree, completes his master's in engineering and opens up his own firm. Sharon stays at home and raises their three kids and does yoga on Tuesdays. On Thursdays, she attends a bible study at her pastor's house. Last Thursday, after bible study, she sticks around and has a few questions for her pastor on his recent sermon on I Corinthians. Unfortunately for Sharon, Pastor Greg has a secret sex addiction and rage toward women, takes advantage of her trust in him by using his position combined with her faith of God and organized religion, and as he lures her into a room alone, he makes a pass at Sharon, which shocks her. She attempts to fight him off, only to stir his aggression, resulting in Pastor Greg raping Sharon. Distraught, she runs out of the house and heads straight for the police station. Her husband Bill meets her there to console her after his frantic wife, with shaky hands, tells Bill to meet her there via the text; "There's been an emergency." Here's how that sounds:

Sharon: I need to file a police report. I've just been violently raped.

Police: OK. (takes out pen and paper). Where were you and who was it that did this felonious crime? Was it a stranger? A friend? Were you on a date?

Sharon: I was at a bible study. *sobbing* My pastor…

Bill: I want justice! *holds Sharron tight and informs police as to what he can make of Sharon's story through her tears, hyperventilating and hysteria*

….After the full story has been relayed to police….

Police: Bill…don't worry. We'll get this scum bag. Take your lovely wife to the hospital to get a rape kit. With that rape kit, we have him by the balls. I assure you sir. Oh, and here's the number to a rape therapist. Tell Dr. Sunshine I sent you. She's amazing. I'm so sorry for what happened to your wife. Here's my card. Let me know if there's anything I can do to help you. I'll see you at the gym.

The contradiction in the two stories is alarming. As a culture have created all types of excuses as to why Sugar "asked for it." However, when women are in the sex for sale trade, because of the mind frame that it's her fault, the intrinsic slut shaming, Sugar knows she doesn't have the "right" to report because it's "her fault." The result of this truth is that women in the commercial sex trade quickly learn that no means yes.

Dear Aspiring Stripper

*The following letter was written by a woman in the commercial sex industry: *

"Dear Aspiring Stripper,

I'm writing you this letter because I wish I had the wisdom of a seasoned dancer presented to me when I entered the industry 8 years ago.... If you think you want to dance for a living, ask yourself why. Is it the rush of doing something counter culture? Are you seeking a different identity to hide behind? Is it the wads of cash you will be going home with? Is it because you want to dance?

Let me first state that: I'm not going to demonize sex work. In fact, sex work/stripping/income exchanged for some level of physical affection is real work, and all sex workers deserve to be respected and recognized in society as any other worker.

There is a pro/con ratio to this industry as any other, but the cons can have a very deep impact on the rest of your life. If you want to get into the club industry ask yourself this instead:

Am I prepared to have intimacy issues with men for the duration of my dancing career, or possibly the rest of my life? Am I prepared to dance 5-7 years longer than I planned to?

Am I prepared to take most of my hopes and throw them down the toilet because that investment $ for that business just never seems to build...? Am I prepared to be desensitized to the slight sexual assaults that happen every time I go to work? (i.e. ass-grabbing, tit-slapping, and god knows what if I bend over) Am I prepared to take on an addiction (i.e. alcohol, cocaine, sex, shopping) to cope with the drastic change in lifestyle?

Am I prepared for the rollercoaster of profiting low one night, to being a top club earner the next? Am I prepared to dissect what part of my body/face/personality isn't good enough because I haven't had a good night in a while? Am I prepared to never see my friends/family because I now sleep during the day? Am I prepared to be ostracized while simultaneously glorified by different fractions of society? For example, ostracized by the "straight" world, glorified by pole dancers that think stripping is getting paid to pole?

Am I prepared to be "saved" by every man who believes that statement in itself is not objectifying? Am I prepared to "retire" from the industry to downgrade to a job with significantly lower income, only to go back because I do not have the qualifications to get a job that requires a salary equal to stripping? (hint: this is a tough one, good luck baby stripper!)

Am I prepared to be out of the job market due to the big hole in my resume? Am I prepared to have no benefits or employment rights? These are just a few things that may run through your mind.

I say this, and I know you're not going to come talk to me because this is none of what you want to hear. I'm really saying this because I hope that if someone sold you the glitz and glory of it, or if you are the person that is doing that, please stop. You never know how much you may be damaging someone's life. So aspiring pole dancer, if you have read all that and still feel you must do this job, come talk to me.
Sincerely,
[Anonymous]"

As you can see, women from the commercial sex industry are a marginalized people group. They are judged, treated differently, and by these examples, we can say they are culturally considered "less than". Women in the commercial sex industry know they don't have the same rights as other women, are not treated the same, are not looked at the same or considered equal to other women, never mind the men.

They are considered and looked at as products to be sold, not people to be respected and loved. Because of that identity, the way they function from the subculture and into the mainstream culture has its own challenges. We must first understand this issue of how these women identify themselves in order to understand their own social cues, and how they got into the industry, and finally, how the mainstream society contributes to the overall problem.

CULTURE

There are many different definitions for the word "culture." To ensure consistency and mutual understanding as we move forward in this next section, we've defined the word *culture* as "what is socially acceptable and non-acceptable within a group of people that governs their agreed perspective about the internal social rules created by the mass majority of those people within that particular cultural group in a given society"[4,5]

Each society has different cultures (i.e. church culture, hip-hop culture, academic culture). Each of these cultures has varying perspectives on society as a whole, and in turn, behaves in a modified way in accordance with their beliefs. Each culture varies in the **paradigm** (i.e. framework) that defines and separates each culture from another. Each paradigm is based on the collective **perspective** (i.e. viewpoint) of the overall society. Within each culture is a distinct agreement to what is "right" and what is "wrong."

Also, we will use the word **subculture** defined as "a group of people within a culture that differentiates itself from the parent culture to which it belongs, often maintaining some of its founding principles."[6]

In order to have the right perspective, one must see the paradigm that eclipses the truth they seek. Only then will the culture create the shift necessary for the safety of the whole—women free from sexual violence. We do that by shedding light on things previously viewed by the wrong perspective causing conclusions about people that have fed the thing we're fighting. Learning something new always comes from asking the right questions.

Rape Culture

The commercial sex culture (i.e. rape culture) is a subculture with an unbalanced, unhealthy high potency of patriarchy. The subculture thrives off of the oppression of women by using greed as its foundation and a perverted power as its roots. Everything and everyone are considered a product of sale; women's sexuality (and children) are considered the highest value or currency. This subculture is set up for the expression of male dominance and asserts this "power-hierarchy" through financial gain, and self-serving, male-gratifying, female sexuality. Nothing is profitable for women in this subculture when they are deemed as objects to be bought and sold instead of people to be loved, respected, and protected.

The way that a woman inside the subculture may talk, think, walk, sneeze and breathe is something that has been conditioned by the subculture, just as the culture was also programmed (i.e. the communication rules of a culture etc.) and is vastly different from the mainstream at large. For example, when women within the subculture use words that are stereotypically offensive to people in the mainstream, it is imperative to understand the true meaning of what is being said. Inasmuch as someone from one culture is aware of the differences in the language, clarity of the meaning behind the message is received. Because of this, women in the subculture are in a sense "bilingual." They've grown up in mainstream, attend public places, function in different facets of mainstream, but they've traveled through the dark tunnel from the mainstream culture by way of trauma into rape subculture that many don't even know exist.

When the awareness hits that they're operating in the rape subculture (once they've been fully indoctrinated into it), culture shock is created within them, and they either have to adjust to the new paradigm or escape it (if that's even a possibility). If they stay, they must learn to navigate through their new culture which is best illustrated in Darwin's Theory of Evolution—Survival of the Fittest.[7] With this in mind, people within the sex for sale subculture must function in a dual-cultural paradigm. Going back into the mainstream paradigm exclusively is no longer an option; it does not exist. They have literally been changed forever. Furthermore, the more they are indoctrinated into the subculture, the more adjustment is required for survival. The equivalent effort is needed when her time of exodus comes. When they return back to the mainstream culture, they should be considered a number-one threat to the status quo; the ones who've overcome the harshest patriarchal climate that exists—the same patriarchy that was built to break them.

Having a working knowledge of how people communicate is one of the main components of any culture. Trying to understand the commercial sex subculture from the same mind frame that we've used for centuries (that stereotypes, assumes and concludes) won't work if our end goal is destroying a system of slavery within our society. **We have to first understand the language and process it through the subcultural paradigm. We cannot process the information through our own cultural interpretation; we will lose the meaning and intent of their message in the translation**. Therefore, it's imperative to obtain the linguistic code from the subculture to assure the intended meaning is received before we report any data, facts, assumptions or conclusions. Otherwise, the information attempted at being obtained is false and perpetuates "numbers" and "facts" that are overly subjective with no working knowledge to base it from. In order to ensure accurate data, metrics, and research, a new paradigm is required. Insofar that this is accomplished, the culture that you have seen to be so inferior, animalistic and poor in thought will be seen in a new light. You will learn a lot about yourself in the process.

COMPONENTS OF THE SUBCULTURE

Time

As defined at the beginning of this section, a subculture has some components similar to the parent culture. Time is clearly the same twenty-four-hour day everyone else has. But it is mentally constructed in a different way—hence why they call it the fast lane. Instead of a concept of time in a linear trajectory where planning exists, and future goals are set on a continuum, days are nights and nights are days, and the only time is now.

There is a consistent, life-threatening awareness that you grow accustomed to and create mechanisms to avoid dangerous situations. The mechanisms you create then provide a narcotic to the emotion of fear that would prohibit you from being able to survive the life in the first place. It's imperative to be able to make a split-second decision, if and when a situation requires you to move and shake free from immediate impending danger. Can you imagine, in the middle of an event which requires you to be hyper-alert, checking your watch? That state of crisis is the consistent state where the perception of time moves faster.

As the above "Letter to an Aspiring Stripper" states, these women are sometimes ostracized from their mainstream family and friends because they are now sleeping during the day and working at night. According to Cathy O'Brien, the author of *Trance Formation of America*, there is no concept of time when the brain has compartmentalized traumas, which leads to fluid movement throughout time.[11]

The overall perception of time in the commercial sex subculture operates in an interesting way; it is something to be observed. The best analogy for how time is perceived in the sex-for-sale culture is the concept and description of a fluid. The fluidity of time feels similar to a rushing river. It is headed somewhere, and your mind focuses on avoiding the threat of drowning or falling headfirst into a waterfall. The overall perception of a twenty-four-hour period differs from the mainstream perception of that same length of time. This in turn creates the illusion that the time feels different (i.e. fast) when in fact, the length of time is the same.

RELATIONSHIPS

One of the most important pieces of any culture is relationships. The interpretation of the male/female dynamic is at the root of everyone's interpersonal relationships regardless of the original experience. Because it is the first relationship (lack of relationship included) each one of us had, it sets the tone for every other relationship; it is the anchor to all other relationships (personal, familial, professional, romantic etc.) In other words, we all got here the same way—it took a male and a female to create us, so all of us have a maternal and paternal experience. Since the foundation of all relationships is built on trust, your internal belief system is created by what you trust to be reality. That reality is the sum total of what life has shown you (positive or negative) to be real. Inasmuch as you've been shown, the internal interpretation and conclusion of reality is programed and leaves you subjected to which paradigm you're most aligned with. The strongest, most consistent experience will become your conclusion.

To state the obvious, the entire rape subculture is founded on the belief that women are objects for sale. In this context, when a woman is subjected to sexual abuse and exploitation consistently, and no experience contradicts the experiences, she trusts that as truth, whereby her belief system is formed. The consistency of abuse is how she defines her relationships. Life has shown her something so often, she trusts that males and females function in this capacity, and no other experience has taught her otherwise. **It is here that she is put in the commercial rape subculture long before she has the capacity to physically and/or mentally agree**. She was a slave before she "chose" to be. Her life experiences repeatedly showed her consistent information with nothing else to override or contradict it. She, as all of us do, trusts what she knows to be true, causing her paradigm to already be in alignment with the sex for sale subculture. Per her experience in mainstream culture, she is an object instead of a person, and she's surprised at the reaction of shock she receives from the relationships she had prior when the people who knew her "can't believe she's having sex for money." Her life however, in mainstream culture, formed her internal reality; the reflection of her truth is found in the subculture.

When something contradicts the truth that life has taught a sex slave, she will reject it as a lie. For example, if the sum total of your experiences teaches you consistently that every time you get up to walk, someone close to you says they love you while simultaneously breaking your legs, the only thing you know is that walking = broken legs and broken legs = love. If someone comes to you and says they love you and asks you to go for a walk, you will either stay seated and kick them out of your house in a fit of anger (nevertheless bound to the chair of fear for the rest of your life) or stand up to walk and when they don't break your legs, you feel rejected and kick them out because you've concluded that they lied about loving you. If no other experience with those ingredients in them have transpired in your life that contradict the original consistent experience where your legs were broken, then both of these outcomes are possible depending on how you conclude. If walking = broken legs, reject anyone who wants you to walk. If breaking your legs = love, when someone refuses to break your legs, they don't really love you—they're lying. You trust the dominant experience over anything else, including your interpretation of something that looks familiar with a one-time contrary outcome. That contrary experience has to be rejected; you can't trust it because it's not real. Herein lies the entire basis for the paradigm of relationships inside rape culture.

In all cultures, all relationships follow the rules within the paradigm of each respective culture. When the consistent experience of all previous relationships is abuse, trauma, rape, exploitation, devastation, she trusts that and the subculture reinforces it and assures her that her belief system is right. She has assigned "love" based on her experiences with what she was told consistently and defines love based on that. She trusts that men will abuse her because no other experience has taught her otherwise. She trusts that those who love her will rape her. Love then, is defined in her head as rape. By default, rape is defined as love. Her worth is her sexuality. Sexuality is all she's worth. The truth she trusts because of what she's been taught is what will lead her decisions, until something contrary happens to challenge it and is consistent enough to prove her wrong. That disillusionment process takes time and a lot of support from people willing to give her new experiences consistently. Until then, she trusts that love looks like rape, she's not a person but an object, and this interrupts any chance at healthy interpersonal connections. The sum total of her experiences with the world at large resulted in the disruption of the ability for healthy interpersonal connection, and her distorted view of what life taught her has her looking at the world upside down.

When someone comes into an agreement that they are an object or are being forced to be seen as an object, the ability to form connections in personal relationships are hindered if not destroyed. Objects cannot form relationships with people. They're objects and don't relate to anything else. The entire culture exists based on the premise that "she" is for sale. The men and women in the subculture agree with this paradigm. To what degree depends on the extent they're indoctrinated into the paradigm. The more indoctrination, the more "successful" you become within the culture. The more "successful" you are at being an object, the more work it takes to prove otherwise and turn your life right-side up again. The effects of the objectification of women in this culture are beyond anything anyone can articulate.

EMOTIONS

Another important component in the subculture is the lack of emotion. In mainstream society, emotions are seen as "weak". We've all culturally agreed that crying is unacceptable and "bad" behavior. We've conditioned our boys not to cry and mock them as weak by comparing them to the product we sell in our society by saying, "Why are you crying like a little girl?" or "Big boys don't cry." We've done this to our little girls too because we've taught them the same; having no emotion is seen as strength. Objects don't have emotions.

How many times do we get into a situation where a woman or a man cries in either a social setting and/or (God forbid) a professional setting, and they say "I'm sorry" when they start to cry. Do they apologize when they laugh? Of course not. Mainstream culture has unconsciously groomed the human experience to be objects. And since objects don't have emotions, it's good to be stoic and bad to be emotional and the definition of strength is "being a man" and "keeping your game face on" which just happen to be the perfect ingredients for grooming sex slaves.

In reality, true strength is being vulnerable. The pure courage it takes to show how you really feel about something is completely undervalued. All humans have emotion—it is part of the human experience. We're taught to think our way out of emotions and stuff them because you "shouldn't" feel or be felt. Interestingly, that is an impossible task; thoughts and feelings come from different parts of the brain. Every emotional response or reaction is rooted in a thought, whether that thought is true or false, but when we're conditioned to deny all emotions, we're weak to be our authentic self because we never take the time to explore what we really believe—our true thoughts. Our emotions are our amazing internal informant that lead us to the real thoughts we don't even realize we have, and it's there we can expose what we really believe and confront the lies that keep us bound.

The illusion we've all been programmed to believe is that women are weak, and emotions are weak. We are conditioned to deny anything feminine, because women are created to be dominated. This entire intrinsic social structure is exaggerated in the trafficking culture. It feeds off denying emotions such as fear, sadness, love, joy, etc. and thrives off of dominating anyone (or in the eyes of the oppressor, anything) that exhibits these characteristics. On a subconscious level, it's an attempt to control the feminine and dominate it even if that means the murder of it.

The subculture breeds on the murderous tendency to snuff out anything they've defined as "feminine". As long as femininity is seen as "weak", we can *exploit it, kill it, conquer it, SELL IT*. But in essence, **there's a huge power in the true feminine equal to the true masculine. They've counterfeited it and misused it so they can sell it.** The problem resides in the fact that women are reduced down to believing their identity as female is something that only serves men: their vagina and sexuality. They are just an object for men to do whatever they want with.

If fear is shown in the rape culture, it is comparable to bleeding in a shark tank. If sadness is shown, it's manipulated for the traffickers' gain. If the emotional make up of a human shuts off, how then will the physiological system of a gut feeling work when someone is in danger? By denying the emotional part of ourselves, we kill the part of our physiological makeup that allows us to navigate out of a world set up to destroy and kill us. This affects not just the women in the culture, but the men as well.

With emotional repression as a foundational survival technique, this repression also feeds into the loyalty construct of the culture. Loyalty over truth plays a big part in rape culture. In order to exist in this world, you learn quickly that there is safety in numbers. Staying loyal to a lie will keep you alive. Breaking loyalty to lies and living your truth will kill you. You cannot survive it.

Culturally, when someone breaks the "rule" of loyalty, the saying is, "Snitches get stitches." A snitch is someone that rats out the illegal activity and breaks loyalty when questioned by law enforcement. Loyalty works as a shackle to keep everything hidden in the dark and the system thriving. Loyalty is a currency. It brings a level of "trust" to a person that, if something happens, they'll keep the secret and die with the lie if necessary. This is seen as a very important cultural value. It is interwoven into the social system of rape culture by believing that loyalty is keeping everyone safe. In a healthy culture, we understand that this is actually keeping everyone enslaved.

Once trapped in the trafficking culture, a conditioning process is used to program women and men. The use of threats serves as a safety net for traffickers from their victims exposing them, and they are rewarded and applauded when they don't break loyalty, even if that reward is they stay alive.

In understanding motive, all decisions can be boiled down in any culture to asking "What then?" or, "Then what?" I do this, then what? I plan on doing this, what then? It reveals true intention. At the very base of every human decision, we find one of two things: love or greed. Love serves others. Greed serves self. Love is a power. Greed is its counterfeit. Love seeks to express truth. Greed seeks to repress, destroy and win. If you comb through all decisions and get to the core motive, you'll find one or the other.

DRUGS

Drug and alcohol use are so prevalent and socially acceptable even within mainstream society. If I have a headache, I take a pain reliever. If someone is hurting, they'll alleviate pain.

However in the sex for sale culture, the pain is much different. It's a pain in their soul—their heart. The rules of engagement, however, say anything that hurts is seen as weakness. So, in order to survive and alleviate any emotional feelings whatsoever, cocaine, heroin, alcohol, meth, molly, acid, etc., etc., etc., is an attempt to continue to function in a culture set up to kill, steal and destroy.

MONEY

In the mainstream culture, money is seen as the determining factor for worth. Social status is based on financial status. Wealth determines more than just the social vote on whether you're deemed as important and worth being respected; it goes much deeper than that. The more money you have, the more you're elevated in the hierarchy where the law has a limit. Most of the decisions rooted in mainstream culture strongly revolve around chasing that mighty dollar. People judge their worth off of their bank account. Our time is spent collecting Benjamin Franklin. It isn't a far stretch then, that as a byproduct of the smog, mainstream culture birthed out a subculture with an exaggerated focus on financial gain that we now officially sell people and then act surprised about how "those people" could do something "so heinous" but we're all sure it "doesn't happen here". That only happens "in other countries" to "those people". As greed sits over the mainstream society like a green smog, suddenly everything turns into an object, and we sell it. Including our children. We as a society then, have been the author in creating this dangerous monster.

Money in the subculture's paradigm essentially has the same meaning as it does in the mainstream. The only variant is in mainstream it's culturally acceptable to make decisions from the viewpoint of love and interpersonal relationships rather than making decisions from the perspective of money. In mainstream, there's a mixture of the two that creates an opportunity for more freedom in the decision-making process.

The entire structure of selling sex is exclusively based on the obtainment and accumulation of the dollar bill. Every decision made is done so with the end goal of money, and always with the agreement that the female object is the "supply" in which to obtain it. No one within this paradigm can exist with love as their "god"; it would contradict the very thing they're after and the agreement of that paradigm of how to obtain it. In other words, if you perceive women as people, you cannot sell them as an object. You'd consider their wellbeing and the effects your decisions regarding them would have before setting something into motion. When love is not a factor, moving the "her" into a mental space of "it" creates the atmosphere for the required end goal.

In the sex for sale culture, the threshold for what extremes it is socially acceptable to go to in order to achieve financial gain is wider than in mainstream. Therefore, crimes are an accepted and expected component; people will do whatever is necessary to achieve financial gain. Nothing is off limits, and there are no rules. This is the main influence in the entire paradigm, and the antithesis and the antidote are those that bravely navigate their lives with love as their compass.

The stereotype existing within the mind frame of the general population is that women within rape culture are incapable of fiscal responsibility or even able to pass high school, nevermind keep a "9-5 like Molly and James who just bought a new modular home only 2 miles from Panera." Their (sex workers) "financial habits" look "plush" and "careless" and "reck-loose" and she's "money hungry" and a "gold digger". "Maybe they're just there because they grew up broke and the money looked appealing," says the patriarchal stereotype.

Upon further digging into the stereotype of why a woman would sell herself for money based on the assumption she's from a poor family, we can give a plethora of examples in which men and women from lower socioeconomic statuses—reaching all the way to poverty and homelessness—have planned, built, executed and successfully climbed out of the "matrix" of the gerbil wheels. What then, is the difference? When it comes to "lower socioeconomic status", the "patriarchy keeps us all chasing a carrot." As long as I can keep up with the Jones, I've arrived. A college degree (debt to pay I'm struggling to work my way out of), a new modular home (mortgage requiring a two income family—spouses are so financially stressed they never see each other, get on each other's nerves, and only stay together for the kids), two-car garage (I can't refinance and my interest payment is so high I had to take out another credit card), and a dog that brings down the value of the home because he's defecated all over the living room carpet. Can't talk now neighbor! Gotta go pick up little Molly from the daycare I had to budget for and make "payment arrangements" just so she can have the organic gummy bears and sit next to Mr. and Mrs. Jones's kids; and chances are, by the time I retire, I'll hate my spouse because they're a stranger, my child is in college now accumulating the same debt I may or may not have gotten out of for a degree I never really needed, and the dog is dead and I'm stuck with this shitty carpet alone in a house I'm still trying to get out from yet another refinance.

This my friends, is the financial shadow that has Americans enslaved. Have we had a minute, before we take our sleeping pill from the doctor who gives us all the medication we need to function through the robotics, to ask ourselves, "Do we realize that maybe the commercial sex industry is just a mirror of what we've become as a society?"

But I digress. On the flip side, within the subculture, money is best described as "quick" just as time is described as "fast". When you're in the fight or flight response, planning ahead isn't an option. The trauma of the industry prohibits sex workers from long-term planning. Furthermore, the brain isn't even fully developed until the age of twenty five, and most sex workers start well under that age (usually in their teens).[12] Therefore, to expect someone from within this culture to engage in long term financial planning and wise financial decisions would be asking someone to perform tasks when they don't even have the fundamental tools to begin with. Furthermore, women that have a trafficker don't manage their own money because it's HIS money; he OWNS her. She has no context on how to handle finances at all and no idea how to get the help she needs to escape. No one is protecting her.

It's not uncommon for cash to be kept in shoe boxes, and spent quickly on expensive items to somehow prove that they are valuable, which is an exaggerated expression of what was taught within the mainstream culture. There is no grid work—no cultural framework—that tells these women that they should be more financially conscious; plan their expenses out. How would they be? No one in mainstream culture realizes they drank from the same Kool-Aid fountain. Instead, there is a subconscious guilt associated with the money they've made just to put food on the table. It's a subconscious guilt that has been programmed into them their entire life—the same script programmed into every one of us. The guilt of being a woman within this industry and how the rest of the world views them is just exaggerated.

As fast as the money is made is as fast as it needs to be spent; saving it isn't an option due to the reality of how it was gained and the guilt that is attached to their false identity which mainstream culture has projected on them. That guilt translates to money, and money translates to the appearance of wealth. Instead, this appearance of wealth is fraudulent, and the perpetrator is the social programming that downgrades women in the concentrated expression of the patriarchal society. We must UNLEARN the patriarchal version of female worth, female pleasure, and female identity in order to see the desperate shift needed in the female destiny.

The root currency in rape culture is power. The access to the illusion of power and the baseline of selling people is money. Therefore, the relationships you foster are monetarily based. When receiving love is the hidden motivator to these women (and the rest of us), and they are taught by their sex-for-sale culture that it will cost them to receive this love—they are willing to do whatever it takes to receive it. Money and sex are the only survival tools women have in this culture; they've been hornswoggled into using something that traumatizes them to gain something that is already available to them in an ideal culture where authenticity of self for both men and women exists.

A mind shift is imperative. In rape culture, a complete absence of love rules. The only love you'll find is the love of power and the only power in rape culture is the motivation for money. Benjamin Franklin is God and you'll do anything to serve him.

In mainstream society, we are conditioned into that same lie—money is your only power. As a result, your choices are limited which prohibits your soul's unique expression, leaving these limited choices to feed things that don't reflect your truth. For example, what if someone was created to be a caregiver and feed babies in Africa dying of AIDS, but they've been raised where the conditional thought was their only value is money? The outcome is, they will go to school, get their degree, take over the family business and die inside never being able to fully express who they are and why they were created. The part of them that is uniquely designed to express itself in a way only they could was never able to fully release because they sold out for "financial stability".

What then, is the difference between that and prostitution? Selling yourself for money is the same. Decisions rooted in loyalty and financial gain at any cost is exactly what we see in the culture of sex for sale. Fundamentally, it's a much more concentrated form, and we see it in a severely exaggerated subculture, but until we revolutionize our own mainstream culture and question what created the atmosphere for this to have space, we are not equipped to change it—to provide freedom for slaves whose lives literally depend on it. Doctors don't perform surgery without clean hands. We shouldn't expect to be effective in solving the problem in a subculture until the world we live in changes and we understand how we've played a part in aiding the breeding ground for this to exist.

We continue in even more detail at unconsciously feeding the climate for rape culture by agreeing that a woman's "worth" has a value system based on things that are socially constructed. We've agreed for decades that a woman's worth is her ability to look like a list of things that can either "do" or "look" or "appear" depending on the era. These measures of value that no one questions are decided the "top shelf", "bottom shelf", "free" ranking that is the byproduct of never understanding the true power of what a woman is in her being. For this era, the most expensive "currency" for selling women is a blonde-haired, blue-eyed, white female (varying according to the year and social propaganda in which media plays a heavy influence i.e. big boobs, no butt in the 1980's, big butt, big boobs in the 2000's etc.) A man identifies his worth as well based on his car, Rolex, and blonde. Intrinsically, we've conditioned little girls into this—even since Barbie was created, who, might I add, has no nipples (and that's just one example). We see the same "ideal" of what sexuality is defined as in the objectification of Marilyn Monroe. In rape culture, you can make way more money off of a blonde-haired, blue-eyed little girl than any other race, because of the control and ideal we've decided is feminine power. If a man can dominate and control the hierarchy of "female", we've set him up to believe he's powerful. In doing so, he can buy his way into an illusion of power that's been intrinsically fed to him since he was a child. Which leads us to a clear picture of who's REALLY vulnerable.

THE VULNERABILITY FACTOR

3. THE VULNERABILITY FACTOR

PRESEASON: ZERO TO SIX

With this vulnerability in mind, it is critical that we focus in on the experiences that a person has in the early developmental stages of their life. How the brain from infancy develops a sense of self, what the effects are on the development of the human brain depending on their environment and how this determines how they see themselves, and what happens when trauma is introduced into the developing brain all play a role in truly understanding the sex-for-sale culture.

Of particular importance in the developing brain is the interaction between the prefrontal cortex and the amygdala. The prefrontal cortex is in charge of evaluating how dangerous something is. In the early development stages of life, the prefrontal cortex builds mental "boxes" that serve as frames of reference for deciding whether something within their immediate environment is dangerous or not. Moreover, during the first six years of our life, our fundamental perceptions about life and our role in it develop without our having the capacity to choose or reject those beliefs.[13] Therefore, what happens in these stages of life is then created as a mental framework of what is "normal".

There is a theory of human development called the Constructivist Self Development Theory.[14] This theory looks at the interaction between a person and what's going on around them. In particular, it looks at the person's sense of self as they mature. The basic belief of the theory is this: how a person interacts with his/her surroundings depends on what happens to her during his/her formative years (ages 0-6). A person's sense and interpretation of "reality" is formulated during these years and can change dramatically depending on what happens to her (Epstein & Erksine, 1983[15], Mahoney, 1981[16]).

As a person grows and develops, they incorporate more and more of their surrounding environment into their existing framework of how the world works (based on the experiences they've had). A person's idea of how the world should function, and what is or is not "normal" is known as their conceptual framework.

In the **object relations theory,** these conceptual frameworks (their "normal") are equivalent to mental representations of the self and of others.[17] In other words, "your" world is a mental representation or sum total of your interpretation of past experiences, as well as your evolving sense of self and how you perceive and experience others.

When changes to this conceptual framework happen, this is called **accommodation and assimilation,** which was first described in Piaget's cognitive development theory (Piaget, 1972).[18]

When the environment that presents new information isn't in agreement with into our existing "boxes" we've believed to be a normal experience, cognitive schemas are modified by a process called **accommodation.**[19] In other words, if an event takes place that does not "fit" within our constructed sense of self and reality, the brain will modify that event so that it adheres to the confines of our interpretation of reality. It is not surprising, then, that our society's existing concept of trauma becomes very convoluted.

Accommodation and assimilation are constantly happening within a person's psyche in early childhood and throughout life. As it occurs, the psychological system matures and differentiates by many factors at play. Psychologists refer to this normal growth and maturation as **progressive self-development.**[20]

THE UTILITY PLAYER: BETRAYAL TRAUMA

When sexual trauma occurs in early development (especially in ages 0-6), there is no way for a female to accommodate or assimilate into healthy sexuality (without proper processing from mental health or family support), because her mind has been programmed to think of her sexuality as something other than a healthy expression of herself with the power to choose how, when, with whom, and why she wants to express it. Her power to choose has been stolen, her frame of reference is distorted, and her "normal" is rape, and she calls it love. Her true sexuality isn't able to be expressed due to the hardwiring of the brain before she can decide what's right and what's wrong. Sexuality is something that's been exploited and abused. Anything besides her "normal" conflicts with her interpretation of reality.

Furthermore, when trauma happens, the victim gets "stuck" physiologically, and what would cause an internal alarm (fight or flight response) to set off and produce a warning that the victim is in danger no longer works; they're stuck in the position of the trauma. This creates the ability to put herself in situations that are also traumatic however she's not alarmed for reasons beyond what she can consciously recall. It feels normal because it's programed in her subconscious as normal. The same situation would cause someone with a healthy list of experiences, which produced a healthy view of self and sexuality, to run for the hills. What is seen as abnormal, unhealthy behavior feels normal to a woman who has experienced this before and is stuck in the fight, flight, or freeze response.

This is how our mind deals with trauma. The identity of self is formed without the ability to realize that sexual abuse is not the norm. Furthermore, between the ages of 0-6, the conscious mind isn't formed yet. Therefore, the brain takes everything in as a sponge and basically says, "This is what life is." By seven, the brain then develops a conscious mind in which "right" and "wrong" are available. Judgements can be made on each event (whether it's the right thing or the wrong thing), but only according to what's already been pre-programmed into the subconscious. Ninety-five percent of our decisions are made from the subconscious (the hard drive of our brains) and the two ways to get something into the subconscious after the age of six is either through *repetition* or *trauma*.[21,22]

From this perspective, we understand that the decisions we believe we're making as a "choice" may not be a result of "choosing" the way we believed. It could be a product of our programming. If we add unprocessed traumatic events that are stored into our subconscious into the equation, we're subject to doing what "seems" normal to us.

In truth however, the ones causing the demise exist in the memory stored in a part of her brain she doesn't even know how to access. She will then blame herself for making decisions where she's set-up to fail...

The System

4. The System

As many times as there is a conference or seminar or training on sex trafficking, someone always asks the question, "What does a trafficker look like?" and inevitably my answer is always, "It looks like you." Words like "pimp" or "trafficker" bring to mind a stereotype that have professionals and members of the mainstream looking for a specific "who" and based on their training or stereotypes, could dismiss what's right in front of their face. The question is not "who" that we need to ask when identifying this crime but "what" is trafficking. The what points to the who.

Trafficking is not a person. It's a system, and that system has infiltrated every other system in the country. Each system, whether it's the political/governmental system, educational system, religious system, familial system, judicial system, entertainment system and every other system that makes up our culture contains the system of trafficking.

With the amount of money that slavery is making, anyone not part of the solution is part of the problem. That statement ranges from turning a blind eye, to being paid off, to financially capitalizing on the sale of sex. When we understand the amount of money this crime is producing, and we understand the subculture, then we can see how it has stayed so prominent and successful for so long. Furthermore we understand how the stereotypes about the women being sold have caused a massive blind spot, limiting our ability to demolish slavery. In other words, if you're trying to dismantle a tapestry, find the string that needs to be pulled. Once you find the string, the entire tapestry will unravel.

Let's look at a few examples in order to confront our preexisting belief system:

1. "One of the most egregious cases involved a three-month-old girl and her 5-year-old sister. **A friend who was staying with the family** offered

to sell them both for sex to an undercover agent from FBI's Denver office for $600."[23]

2. "A third Ohio **pastor** has been indicted on sex trafficking charges, and prosecutors say all three men worked together to entice underage girls with money in exchange for sex."[24]

3. "A former NYPD **officer** was arrested Tuesday for running a prostitution ring. Although he had been on the force for 11 years, the cop allegedly began pimping out prostitutes immediately after his shift ended.[25]

4. Gregory W. Hart of Johnson City, TN — trafficking a person for commercial sex act (felony A) $100,000 **[retired]** Bradley **[landscaping]**Samuel Adam McMurry, of Johnson City, TN – trafficking a person for commercial sex act and trafficking a person for commercial sex act [Washington County, TN **EMT]**Brandon R. Summey, – trafficking a person for commercial sex act **[Dick's Sporting Goods, Bristol, TN, head football coach Sullivan North Middle, Asst. baseball coach Sullivan North High, substitute teacher]**Jose Alejandro Rivero, – trafficking a person for commercial sex act **[Food City Baker, Johnson City Schools food services]**Matthew S. Still- trafficking a person for commercial sex act and trafficking a person for commercial sex act, and sexual battery – **[Customer service at AT&T; and Youth Minister at Restoration Church in Bristol, TN]**Chris K. Ginley, -trafficking a person for commercial sex act and trafficking a person for commercial sex act – **[unemployed]** Kevin J. White, – trafficking a person for commercial sex act (**[installer]**[26]

5. "A Katy Elite **Volleyball coach** was arrested as part of a multistate sex trafficking operation. Wan Yun faces a charge of prostitution, according to charging documents. Other **high profile names were arrested as well, including a well-known sports agent.**"[27]

6. "**High school coach** arrested for pimping after panicked 17-year-old calls 911

The coach, who holds a teaching credential, is listed as having had worked as a **substitute teacher and instructional aide.** . He also has worked as a **coach and referee** in various local youth soccer leagues in the area. His Facebook page shows numerous pictures of both boys and girls teams, although it's not clear which teams he coached. The Sheriff's Department also reported that Seagraves worked as a **driver for both Uber and Lyft.**[28]

7. "Those arrested in police raids have included **school teachers, police officers, law students and sports coaches."**[29]

8. "A U.S. man in Tennessee who **sold his three daughters** to a man who raped them and used them in child pornography has been sentenced to life in prison. According to court records, **both parents** were involved with the abuse and exploitation of the children and were indicted in 2013."[30]

9. "A local **surgeon** is facing human trafficking and other charges for allegedly trying to have sex with a minor. He was arrested during an undercover operation."[31]

10. "A 48-year-old **doctor** is facing charges of prostitution, resisting, obstructing, assaulting police and using a computer to commit a crime."[32]

11. "**Jerry Sandusky's Behavior** Former Pennsylvania State University Assistant Football Coach, Jerry Sandusky, publicly admitted to showering with young boys, giving hugs, touching legs, "horsing around," and snapping butts with towels. That is what he PUBLICLY admitted. He insisted he was not a pedophile and was teaching the boys basic hygiene. The behaviors that Sandusky alluded to are identical to the sexual grooming behaviors of pedophiles.

THE STEREOTYPE OF THE SEX TRAFFICKER:

"When I was young, sex predators were described as disheveled, dirty old men, flashers in raincoats, and perverts hanging around schoolyards."[33] *Dateline NBC-TV's To Catch A Predator* series reveals a more complex picture.[34] The television program uses an organization called the *Perverted Justice Foundation*.[35] Their whose mission is to track down, expose and get convictions of adults **who groom children** online.[36] For the TV show, *Perverted Justice* has adults pretending to be young teens in an effort to open up communication with men targeting them for rape.[37]

In order to understand the system, we have to identify the working parts of the system. Understanding that this issue starts with the predators preying on our children, we now exchange the word "pedophile" for the word "groomer." Let's take a look at the identification and profile of a groomer.

Grooming

According to research from Carla van Dam, Ph.D. in her book, *Identifying Child Molesters*, after interviewing more than 300 convicted groomers she identified specific commonalities.[38] One observation they all had in common was that "many took pride in how they stalked, inveigled and violated young victims."[39] She also discovered that pedophiles have no common physical characteristics, religious preference, no specific race, social class, economic status or profession, and there was no psychological commonality that threaded a common denominator.[40]

She did find things groomers share in common. Of the over 300 she interviewed, the groomers sought vocational positions, either paid or volunteer, for activities where children are present.

She reported that groomers are

"strategically placed in systems where they have access to teach, coach, lead-counsel, care-give and control children. They target single mothers to have access to their children. Ninety-three percent of groomers are someone the child knows. Other groomers target their victims by visiting social places where children are left without protection. They frequent malls, bus stops, public bathrooms, parks, etc.—places which would be obvious to our culture. This is where we've looked for pimps to find our kids. They leave notes on bulletin boards for jobs or modeling, elicit kids on the Internet, or drive around searching for places where kids are found alone. Often they will stalk a victim and observe their habits when they walk home from school. In the Champaign-Urbana area of Illinois during the past several months, nine children were nearly abducted while walking home after school. One man was arrested but was let go because they couldn't locate the witness."[41]

In order to have access, groomers don't just groom the children. They groom the adults as well. They strategically plan and watch where the blind spot is to gain access to the children adults are responsible for protecting. According to Doctor van Dam, "They groom parents, family, friends, teachers, lawyers, neighbors, social workers, counselors, and even police officers and judges. Child molesters must groom the adult community to gain access to a child victim. Considerable thought and planning goes into the process."[42]

Dr. van Dam reports another case: "I read court documents concerning a nine-year-old patient who had the most severe Posttraumatic Stress I've ever seen in a child. Her mother took the father to court multiple times over a five year span, trying to get his visits revoked. The transcript described tongue-to-tongue touching, rolling in bed games, weekends in motels, sleeping in the same bed, burns, serious injuries, severe rashes, lack of supervision and gross neglect."[43]

Aware of this, the judge commented in court, 'He's not a child molester. He's an immature, uninformed father."[44] In one of the proceedings, a teacher, social worker, counselor and psychiatrist testified on the father's behalf. "The father hired a father's rights lawyer to bamboozle the court."[45] She continues on, "...And when the predator is **high profile, a professional, good looking, he can charm anybody into believing anything, no matter the evidence against him.** Fortunately for the child in this case, the father lied to his attorney about major issues of the case. As a result, his lawyer dumped him and the judge revoked his visitation rights."[46]

Here we see how this system is working. The groomer gains access to the "product." He conditions the child through trauma, and when discovered, a cover-up is already set up where people are paid off and turn a blind eye off charm, ignorance, excuses that lead them to financial gain. If you're not part of the solution, you're part of the problem. It's imperative we know how this system is working.

It's been reported that psychopaths, serial killers and pedophiles/groomers share the same personality profile:

"They are notoriously successful in gaining cooperation from people they plan to exploit. Like Ted Bundy, they are opportunistic, intrusive, charming, superficial, and appear too good to be true. They have a compelling, almost irresistible desire to have sex with children. They are intrusive and violate boundaries of privacy and personal space. They're constantly involved with managing their self-image and thinking about what move to make next. They give, but ask nothing in return. They are overly attentive to children and try to spend an inordinate amount of time alone with them. Some pedophiles idolize children and consider them objects to possess or projects to work on. They often use strange, inappropriate words to describe children, such as pure, divine, heavenly or angelic. Having few peer relationships, they prefer the company of children and engaging in child activities, kind of like Peter Pan. Except with foul and nefarious motives". . . "Pedophiles attempt to blur boundaries of what is appropriate, inappropriate, normal or abnormal. They sidle up to a child and invade their body space to gauge the child's resistance or reluctance to being in close physical contact." –Dr. Carla van Dam [47]

Their mode of operation is to desensitize the child to touch is gradual. It increases in various types of touch. Nearly all molesters engage children in tickling, roughhousing, picking the child up, massaging, cuddling, holding, patting, rocking, kissing and touching. That's what Sandusky did. By "accident," pedophiles touch the buttocks, breasts or genitals and just happen to open the bathroom door when the child's inside."[48] This breakdown is then sealed with the mental conditioning the victim of secrecy, which is why loyalty is of such high value in the subculture.

The groomer introduces "secrecy to gain cooperation, participation and silence. The secret isolates the child from freely communicating to others. The predator first introduces insignificant secrets, such as not telling about a movie they saw or an ice cream cone they shared. Secrecy is an ongoing theme and a method of manipulating the child's mind. Pedophiles use threats and violence to intimidate children into silence by telling them:

"This is our secret."

"No one will believe you."

"It's your fault."

"They'll send you away."

"I'll go to prison."

"You'll break up the family."

"I'll hurt your family."

"I'll kill your pet."

"I'll kill you."[49]

This makes it the child's burden and fault; the beginning of self-blame and slut shaming. In another report:

"As early as 2004, school officials reprimanded Jon White for viewing pornography on a classroom computer, but no one contacted authorities or dug deeper to see what this teacher was up to. A mother complained that her daughter said that White had girls give him back rubs under his shirt, and had them rub his legs under his pants."[50] But, incredibly, **the mother was ignored by an Assistant Principal who, despite the damning evidence, stood up for White and insisted he was an outstanding teache**r. In 2008, White was sentenced to 60 years in prison. **Some school officials were fired**, and now millions of dollars in lawsuits are pending against the school district. Why? Because cowardly school officials refused to acknowledge what was going on in front of them. They refused to stand up for the children."[51]

This is not to say that all pedophiles are groomers by being paid off; not all of them are necessarily aware that their sickness leads to a system of trafficking. However, even though ignorance can be innocent, it's costly. We know that pedophiles who are molesting children for their own sick twisted gain have a "type" of child they target. It must be stated and cannot be ignored however, that when a pedophile is exposed, if they have victims that don't fit a "type" (i.e. race, age, body type etc.), he, and others, are using his sickness for financial gain and mass producing "product" to be sold. **Sometimes, what's disguised as "ignorance" is really a ploy for financial gain.** We can see that in the athletic sex scandals being uncovered in the news today.

The legal definition of sex trafficking is defined as "someone using force, fraud, or coercion to cause a commercial sex act with an adult or causes a minor to commit a commercial sex act.[52] It is a system that's been ignored in spite of the evidence of trafficking that has been right in front of our faces.

COLLEGE SPORTS AND TITLE IX

Within the system, there are moving parts. The groomer, the timer, the trafficker, the security, all the way up to the top. College sports in an educational institution, are a notorious breeding ground for sexual crimes against women. The false sense of masculinity is at play here; by sexualizing women, you're defined as a "man." College sports recruiting is notorious for using strippers and prostitutes for bartering on a college visit.[53]

By getting the top recruit, enrollment will increase and the dollars for that school skyrocket. There is a major breakdown, however, when the gas to the car is the selling of women and young girls to pay for the preference of whatever the recruit or best athlete's appetite requires. Remember, this isn't about sex, but about power and control. Power and control are rooted in the patriarchal lies that the system perpetuates.

TITLE IX

Title IX is a federal law in the United States for the educational system that prohibits gender discrimination.[54] It also addresses sexual violence, and legally requires schools to address and eliminate any hostile environment or sexual violence on campus.[55] In the past, failure to do so could result in a risk of losing federal funding.[56,57,58]

To ensure the law is being properly executed, colleges have a Title IX Director, Deputy, Coordinator and/or Investigator.[59] The Title IX Director is employed by the university and takes appropriate actions should the complaint of sexual assault or gender discrimination occur on campus.[60] Off campus assaults involving students however are reported to the campus or local police, and although the school would be notified, it is not required for them to report these cases to federal law enforcement.[61] Therefore, these off-campus incidents are not reflected in national statistics for incidence of sexual discrimination and violence. As a result, any off campus violence doesn't affect the amount annual federal funding that the university receives.[62]

To understand the pay scale of the Title IX Director, here's an example:

Title IX Coordinator Salary [63]

Coordinator Salary	$31,860 - $59,825
Bonus	$0.00 - $5,019
Profit Sharing	$0.00 - $3,860
Commission	$0.00 - $6,478
Total Pay	$30,345 - $57,549

Title IX Investigator Salary [64]

Investigator Salary	$36,588 - $125,550
Bonus	$0.00 - $15,319
Profit Sharing	$0.00 - $24,917
Total Pay	$34,249 - $127,599

Association of Title IX Administrators- 2015 survey of more than 400 institutions higher-ed[65]

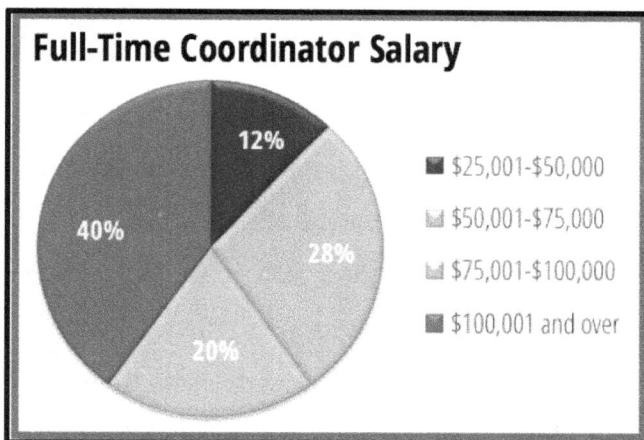

Full-Time Coordinator Salary

- 12%
- 40%
- 28%
- 20%

- $25,001-$50,000
- $50,001-$75,000
- $75,001-$100,000
- $100,001 and over

[66]

- **"Gender**
  - 26% Male
  - 74% Female
- **Training Frequency (Coordinator)**
  - Monthly 3%
  - Quarterly 13%
  - Semi-annually 24%
  - Annually 42%

- 10% of schools in the Association of Title IX Administrators survey indicate that they have full-time Title IX Coordinators who don't have any other primary job responsibilities beyond Title IX roles
- 60% of schools that participated in the survey allow someone to overrule a decision made or approved by Title IX Coordinator
- 51% of schools surveyed reported that they have no budget dedicated to Title IX compliance efforts
- 80% of surveyed Title IX Coordinators have held their job duty for less than three years[67]

Based on these statistics and data, it appears that the people in charge of Title IX are highly paid yet under-trained, and each administrator has different guidelines based on each individual educational institution. There is no consistency. Their position holds power simply because they hold the key to the final decision on whether perpetrators of sexual violence are held accountable for their actions. They also dictate the result of the exposure or cover-up each reported case receives.

The importance and power of this position without highly regulated reporting is questionable and easily used as the rudder to steer and/or manipulate the ship in any case where sexual violence is transpiring on campuses. By default, the administrator also dictates what college athletes, faculty, and students get away with if they are the perpetrator.

Let's look at an example of how this position is put into play and how a system of trafficking can be easily executed right under our noses.

MSU's Very Own: Larry Nassar

In February of 2017, a story broke out involving the Michigan State University Gymnastics team.[68] The physician who tended to the Michigan State athletes, Dr. Larry Nassar, also served as the physician for the USA Gymnastics team. Reports started to come through accusing Dr.

Nassar of sexually assaulting young girls and college athletes during routine visits and exams.[69]

Here are the facts:

THE BACKSTORY:

From 1985-1989 Nassar worked as a graduate assistant athletic trainer at Wayne State University while enrolled in a master's degree program.[70] He dropped out when he was accepted to medical school at Michigan State University.[71] In 1988 Nassar began working with John and Kathryn Geddert, who later open Gedderts' Twistars USA Gymnastics Club in Dimondale, Michigan.[72] In 1993 Mr. Nassar received his Osteopathic Medical Degree from Michigan State University.[73] **Simultaneously, a gymnast reported that Nassar began to sexually abuse her in 1994,** which continued for six years.[74]

All the while Larry Nassar's career advanced, in 1997 he became a team physician and assistant professor at MSU.[75] He was also a team physician at Holt High School and a team physician and assistant professor at MSU.[76] During this time, **a parent raised concerns to John Geddert about Nassar,** but **Geddert didn't notify police.**[77] Within the year, a report was filed against Mr. Nassar; **he began sexually abusing the six–year–old daughter of a family friend.**[78] According to police records, Nassar penetrated her vagina with his fingers "every other week for five years."[79] **In the same year, a student–athlete at MSU reported concerns regarding Nassar to trainers or coaches, but the university "failed to take any action."**[80] Just two years following, **in 2000 a second student–athlete at MSU reported Nassar to trainers or coaches, and again the university "failed to take any action."**[81] During the denial from MSU, Nassar was attending the Olympic Games in Sydney, Australia, with gymnastics teams.[82] Rachael Denhollander, a gymnast who would later file a criminal complaint against Nassar, says she was **sexually abused by Nassar during treatments for lower back pain in 2000.**[83]

She was 15 at the time. **Both the Olympic gymnastics training center AND the university were informed, and nothing was done about it.**[84]

By 2004, Nassar's mass production of traumatization and grooming continued. He'd been reported of obtaining child pornography and abusing a young lady in Ingham County, Michigan.[85] **Her parents, being fully informed of the abuse, did report it.**[86] Even after these consistent allegations, he wasn't questioned however more access was given to him and he attended the 2008 Olympic games in China.[87]

The dam started to break in 2014 after a MSU graduate filed the ever-echoing complaints. **Dr. Nassar sexually assaulted her during a medical examination. Michigan State, however, immediately cleared Nassar of any wrongdoing just three months later.**[88] Even with these complaints, Nassar continued to work even though he was under investigation. The master groomer stayed on staff as top Doctor for the Michigan State gymnastics team.[89] In September 2015, he stepped down as the Olympic physician, however, Everything changed in March of 2016 for Dr. Nassar when The Indianapolis Star published their findings in an investigation they conducted on USA Gymnastics, (which serves as the governing body for the U.S Olympic Gymnastics team).[90]

Per their findings, "**USA Gymnastics has followed a policy of not reporting** all **sexual abuse** allegations **against its coaches.** That practice has **enabled coaches to continuing preying on children despite repeated warning signs**."[91] IndyStar continued that the violations on children "despite warnings of inappropriate behavior."[92] Their groundbreaking report stated that "**at least 368 gymnasts have alleged sexual abuse over the past 20 years. IndyStar also brought to light accusations of sexual abuse by the former team doctor for USA Gymnastics.**"[93]

On August 29, 2016 **another gymnast filed a complaint - this time criminal - with MSU Police.**[94] Her statement was that starting in 2000, at age 15, **she was sexually abused by Nassar during treatments** for lower back pain.[95] Just a day later on August 30th, years after this was first reported, MSU relieved him of all clinical and patient duties and officially on September. 20, 2016 and fired Nassar from his position as an associate professor in the College of Osteopathic Medicine.[96]

If we identify Dr. Nassar as the groomer in the information proceeding, we can see more clearly how the trafficking system works.

Stuart Dunnings III

In an investigation on Nassar in 2014, **Michigan State University referred the police reports over to Ingham County prosecuting attorney Stuart Dunnings III.**[97] Despite the evidence and police reports, **Dunnings "dropped all charges."**[98] In less than two years' time, **Dunnings III (who was considered an expert on the sex trafficking** and exploitation epidemic that was new to the fore front of the state of Michigan) **headlined the news** with the title of the article reading, **"Human Trafficking Investigation Results In Criminal Charges Against Ingham County Prosecutor Stuart Dunnings."**[99]

Here's how the newspaper headline reads:

"Michigan Attorney General Bill Schuette, joined by Ingham County Sheriff Gene Wriggelsworth, today announced the filing of criminal charges against Ingham County Prosecutor Stuart Dunnings III."[100]

The charges were filed at four courts in three Michigan counties (Ingham, Clinton, and Ionia) and include a **total of 15 criminal counts.**[101] **Here's how the charges read:**

"PROSTITUTION/PANDERING, 1 COUNT

- Did induce, persuade, encourage, inveigle or entice a person to become a prostitute, contrary to MCL 750.455 = Felony, 20 years

ENGAGING IN THE SERVICES OF PROSTITUTION, 10 COUNTS

- Did engage or offer to engage the services of a person for the purpose of prostitution contrary to MCL 333.5129 = Misdemeanor, 93 days and/or $500

WILLFUL NEGLECT OF DUTY, 4 COUNTS

- Did willfully neglect to perform his duty to refrain from blatant violations of the criminal law, a duty enjoined on him by his oath of office as a county prosecutor, contrary to MCL 750.478 = Misdemeanor, 1 year and/or $1,000"[10]

CASE BACKGROUND

The charges against Stuart Dunnings grew out of a federal investigation into a Michigan-based human trafficking ring **which took place in 2015** placing the time span between his dismissal of Nassar and the beginning of the investigation within a year.[103] The U.S. Attorney for the Western District of Michigan filed federal charges in that case against human **trafficking ring leader Tyrone Smith** who pleaded guilty on three counts of sex trafficking **young girls and women, including one minor.**[104] **Members of the Michigan Attorney General's Office, FBI, and Ingham County Sheriff's Office** jointly conducted an additional investigation based on information provided by witnesses in the federal investigation of Smith, which led to Stuart Dunnings.[105]

The state-local-federal investigation resulted in evidence that Stuart Dunnings III paid for commercial sex (engaging in prostitution) hundreds of times with multiple women, **between 2010 – 2015,** now placing the timeline in tandem with his ruling on Dr. Nassar. Furthermore, evidence showed that **Dunnings also allegedly induced a woman to become a prostitute** (an identical description of a trafficker—i.e. Force, fraud or coercion) who had not previously been one.[106] Instead of trafficking however, **they charged him with Pandering,** which the dictionary defines as "a person who furnishes clients for a prostitute or supplies persons for illicit sexual intercourse; procurer; pimp."[107] Below are the list of charges and their consequences:

- "1 count, Pandering, **20 years**

    5 counts, Engaging the Services of Prostitution, **93-days and/or $500**

1 count, Willful Neglect of Duty, **1 year and/or $1,000**

- 2 counts, Engaging the Services of Prostitution, **93-days and/or $500**

  1 count, Willful Neglect of Duty, **1 year and/or $1,000**

- Engaging the Services of Prostitution, **93-days and/or $500**

  1 count, Willful Neglect of Duty, **1 year and/or $1,000**

- Engaging the Services of Prostitution, **93-days and/or $500**

  1 count, Willful Neglect of Duty, **1 year and/or $1,000**"[108]

The article reads, "**Dunnings has served as Ingham County Prosecutor since 1997 and has been an outspoken advocate for ending human trafficking and prostitution.**"[109]

At the announcement in Lansing, officials offered the following comments:

ATTORNEY GENERAL BILL SCHUETTE:

- "Human trafficking is a crime that puts people, in this case young women, into situations where their lives are endangered and where they are manipulated and brutalized. During an investigation into a suspected human trafficking ring, **we discovered that one of our own was using the services of women who were being trafficked.**"[110]

I'd love to ask, "Why did the Attorney General's Office charge him with 'pandering' instead of 'trafficking', especially with the 24 laws implemented by Senator Judy Emmons. Surely we should call this what it is seeing he was so involved in the investigation. I'd also like to highlight the rhetorical 'why', in his statement, he only alludes to identifying Dunnings as a John. Why not identify Dunnings as the trafficker in which his charges confirm?"

- "We live in a time where people wonder if government actually works. People wonder if the system is rigged. People wonder whether we have a 'wink and a nod' justice system where the chosen few skate and escape punishment because of who they know or because they hold an important position in government. Well, let me be very direct and crystal clear. The system in Michigan is not rigged. Not on my watch."[111]

I'd also like to ask, "After the outcome of conviction and the charges given to Mr. Dunnings, is it fair to say that anyone questioning the legitimacy of the system in reference to 'escaping punishment because of who they know or because they hold an important position in government' is that far-fetched? After the charges he faced and the sentencing he received, I'd like to understand how that's not exactly what happened here. Could someone in the Attorney General's Office explain?"

- **"A personal comment. I have worked with Stuart Dunnings while I have served as Attorney General.** I am saddened that an elected official who holds a special trust from voters and is the chief prosecutor in our capital city would allegedly engage in conduct causing felony and misdemeanor charges to be filed."[112]

These are three very strange comments from someone who then went on to promote his own campaign in the article—the Attorney General concluded his statement with a full advertisement about his work and how to contact his office, etc. It appears as if he has taken an opportunity to promote his career. Self-promotion of one's occupation in a story involving a trafficking ring seems to say the focus on the true victim has been lost. I'd like to ask, "Why are you pointing out that people trusted Dunnings while he was running for Prosecuting Attorney? Are you implying that the victims are the ones who trusted him and voted for him?"

INGHAM COUNTY SHERIFF GENE WRIGGELSWORTH:

- "Engaging in criminal behavior while serving as the Ingham County Prosecutor is a betrayal to everyone in our county that has voted for Mr. Dunnings over the last several decades. **His alleged**

behavior is not what best represents law enforcement in

Ingham County or law enforcement anywhere in Michigan."[113]

As we study further, we will see Mr. Wriggelsworth is incorrect in his
assumed representation of what Michigan Law looks like. Also, his
betrayal is also to the women he violated. Is anyone going to protect
them and use their position to talk about the crime he committed and the
damage he caused the victims? Again, who are the real victims? The
public? Or the victims of his "pandering".

FBI SUPERVISORY SENIOR RESIDENT AGENT TED DOCKS
PROVIDED THIS COMMENT:

- "Through the course of investigating a human trafficking case with
  our partners from the Ingham County Sheriff's Office, **we**
  developed information we could not ignore involving a public
  official. **Although that information did not reach the threshold**
  for a federal violation, we shared that information with the
  Michigan Attorney General's Office. **This sort of interagency**
  coordination is routine to ensure crime problems in the
  Lansing area are addressed appropriately."[114]

Mr. Docks. Why would you ignore any of this? What's the threshold for
a federal violation? The prosecutor was responsible for a sexual assault
case with a groomer from one of the largest trafficking rings this
country has seen, dismissed charges and freed a man who continued to
commit sex crimes on women whose lives will never be the same. That's
not a federal offense? Furthermore, are you promoting your interagency
coordination and giving you and your colleagues a pat on the back?

All three of those men, with the platform to change the culture and
viewpoints on the women they are paid to protect and say they fight for,
had an opportunity to influence the public on how this crime on our
women has to stop. They could have addressed the victims and made an

example out of Mr. Dunnings. The following is an account of the Affidavit. The result of sentencing follows.

Let's take a look at a few key points that are on the affidavit for Mr. Dunnings:

"THE COMPLAINING WITNESS, ON INFORMATION AND BELIEF, SAYS:

1. I , Affiant AMBER KENNY-HINOJOSA, am a detective with the Ingham County Sheriff Department. I have been a certified Michigan police officer since August 1998, and have served as a detective since January 2013. My job duties include the investigation of possible criminal acts as assigned by the department.

2. In the regular course of my duties I was assigned to participate in a joint federal-state investigation into allegations that suspect TYRONE SMITH was involved in human trafficking activities. That investigation led to Sex Trafficking charges initiated in the United States District Court for the Western District of Michigan as United States of America v Tyrone Smith, Case # 1:15-cr - 00 135-RJJ.

3. During the course of the Tyrone Smith investigation the federal-state law enforcement team identified numerous women associated with this charged sex trafficker as present or former prostitutes. Interviews of those persons led to additional persons being identified a s present or former prostitutes. Among those persons being so identified as prostitutes are women here designated as prostitutes W-1, W-2 , W-3. W-4, W-5. The investigation also led to a person who, although she had never before engaged in prostitution, was persuaded to exchange sexual acts in exchange for cash. That person is herein referred to as W-6.

4. Stuart Dunnings III is the duly elected Prosecuting Attorney for Ingham County, Michigan, and has served in this position since January 1997. As the elected Prosecuting Attorney, Stuart Dunnings III is the **chief law enforcement officer for the county**. As the chief law enforcement officer

for the county, he has **a continuing duty imposed by law to refrain from intentionally and blatantly violating provisions of the criminal code.**

5. Steven Dunnings is a licensed Michigan attorney, who was admitted to the State Bar of Michigan in February 1984. He is the brother of Prosecuting Attorney Stuart Dunnings III.[115]

6. In Spring 2010, W-1 posted herself as a prostitute on the internet website Escort Vault. Stuart Dunnings III called her in response to her post, and later that day they met for commercial sex at the Red Roof Inn in Lansing. **Dunnings paid W-1 $200 for this sexual encounter.**

7. For the next 5 years , Dunnings continued see W-1 for commercial sex. They often met for sex as many as **three to four times per week**. Dunnings III took W-1 to hotels and motels in the Lansing area. Separate incidents of commercial sex occurred in the City of Lansing and in DeWitt Township.

8 . Dunnings III has **paid W-1 's rent and given her money on occasions not directly connected to sex acts.** At one point in time, Dunnings III told W-1 that he wanted to be her exclusive customer. W-1 declined this offer. During nearly all of this time, W-1 was using heroin.

9 . Dunnings III desired to have sex with two women at the same time, and he asked W-1 to arrange that. W-1 introduced Dunnings III to W-2 , and all three engaged in commercial sex. On at least one occasion, W-1 briefly **videotaped one of their commercial sex transactions.**

10 . **W-2 met Stuart Dunnings III through W-1 in 2011**. At the time, W-2 was posting as a prostitute on the internet site Escort Vault. Dunnings III called W-2 and **took her to lunch.** The next time they met, Dunnings III and W-2 had commercial sex at a Lansing motel. **W-2 's fees were $100 per half hour, $16 0 per hour, and $140 per hour for multiple hours.** Dunnings III **typically gave her a couple hundred dollars per occasion.** Early into the relationship, Dunnings III told W-2 he was the Ingham County Prosecutor.

11. W-2 continued commercial sex dates with Dunnings III **on a regular basis**. They had commercial **sex over 200 times**. Their meetings **typically involved going to dinner and then going to a motel.** Sometimes Dunnings III did not have time to take W-2 to dinner and would only pick up W-2 and take her to a hotel or motel. Dunnings III usually called W-2 to schedule the time to meet, which was often on a Tuesday. Dunnings III often came to W-2 's house later the same day.

12 . When they first began having commercial sex, **Dunnings III paid W-2 each time following the sexual activity.** As their relationship progressed, Dunnings III **sometimes gave W-2 money for her general use.** Dunnings III **purchased clothing for W-2 , paid her cellular phone bill, took her grocery shopping, and paid her membership at the YMCA.**

13 . After knowing Dunnings III for about six months, **W-2 told Dunnings III she was addicted to heroin. Dunnings III paid about $80 per week for W-2 's methadone treatments.** Dunnings III sometimes attended Narcotics Anonymous meetings with W-1 and W-2. **Around this time, the Lansing Police arrested W-2 and she was charged with possession of drug paraphernalia. Dunnings III took money to W-2 's mother to pay for W-2 's bond.**

14. During the period from 2011 through 2015, Stuart Dunnings III engaged in commercial sex with W-2 at various locations, including the City of Lansing, DeWitt Township, The City of Okemos, and the City of Portland.

15. **In early 2014, W-3 posted on the website Backpage.com. Stuart Dunnings III called W-3 and arranged commercial sex date.** Stuart Dunnings III and **W-3 had commercial sex approximately five times, each time for $200.** The two communicated via cell phone and text. **W-3 responded to all of her calls and texts because her pimp would beat her if she did not respond.** Stuart Dunnings III told W-3 to call him back

at his office. When W-3 called, the line was answered as the Ingham County Prosecutor's Office and W-3 was transferred to Dunnings III .

16. About one week following the initial encounter with Stuart Dunnings III, W-3 had her first commercial sex date with Steven Dunnings. Steven Dunnings identified himself as an attorney, and told W-3 his brother Stuart was the Ingham County Prosecuting Attorney. W-3 and **Steven Dunnings had commercial sex about six or seven times**. On one occasion, **Steven Dunnings asked W - 3 's pimp for permission to take W - 3 to a certain motel because Steven did not like the pimp's preferred motel.**

17 . **W-3 was routinely beaten by her pimp, and throughout the time she had commercial sex with Stuart Dunnings III and Steven Dunnings she had observable bruising on her body. W-3 also had multiple, visible needle tracks on her arms from heroin use.**

18. Some of these separate incidents of commercial sex between W-3 and Stuart Dunnings III and Steven Dunnings occurred in the City of Lansing.

19. W-4 began working as a prostitute because she was a heroin and crack cocaine user and needed money. **Her pimp provided her drugs in exchange for her work, imprisoned her in his house , and beat her. On one occasion, he beat her so severely that W-4 could barely walk and was unable to open her eye for several days. W-4 frequently had bruises on her body that would have been visible to her customers.**

20. **In early 2014, W-4 and W-3 met Stuart Dunnings III at the Magnuson Hotel in Lansing for commercial sex.** W-4 and W-3 **met with Stuart Dunnings III a second time approximately three weeks later at her pimp's house in Lansing.** During the second meeting, Dunnings III told W-4 he was the county prosecutor.

21. W-4 frequently had commercial sex with Steven Dunnings, and **she considered him a regular customer.** This commercial sex occurred at several locations in the City of Lansing.

22. W-5 met Stuart Dunnings III in Spring 2015, **while she was working for a pimp**. Dunnings III responded to W-5 's advertisement as a

prostitute on the website Backpage.com. **Dunnings III paid W-5 $150 for approximately 15 minutes of commercial sex at her apartment in Holt, Michigan.** This was the only incident of commercial sex between the two of them.

23. In 2010, **W-6 was involved in a custody dispute with the father of her child. She sent an email to Stuart Dunnings III, seeking assistance in this custody matter. Dunnings III responded, and had W-6 meet him at his office. W-6 advised Dunnings III that she had been the victim of domestic violence, and that the father of her child was the person who assaulted her.**

24. **After discussing the custody matter, Dunnings III invited W-6 to lunch at a café in a downtown Lansing hotel. She accepted the offer and had lunch with him. They parted right after the lunch, and W-6 did not give the matter much thought.**

25. Shortly thereafter, Dunnings III invited W-6 to lunch a second time. That lunch occurred in the City of Lansing. During that second lunch, **Dunnings III noted that he was aware that W-6 was struggling financially, and that he had a proposition for her. Dunnings III advised W-6 that he was seeking a sexual relationship with her, and that he would pay her money in return.**

26. W-6 was initially shocked by this proposition and **did not immediately accept.** After thinking the proposition over, **she felt she had no choice but to accept.** W-6 then began an on- and-off **one to two-year commercial sex relationship with Dunnings III.** W-6 estimates that **Dunnings III paid her about $600 every two weeks during the times they would meet for commercial sex.** In addition to giving W-6 cash, he also provided her with gifts and paid some of her bills.

27. **Dunnings III 's position as the Ingham County Prosecutor influenced W-6's decision to engage in commercial sex with him. She both hoped that he would help her in her child custody dispute and feared that he might cause her problems if she refused his proposition.**

While W-6 had no adult arrests or drug use, **she was afraid that he might make up something negative to hurt her if she did not go along.** W-6 asserts that she would not have gone along with the commercial sex if Dunnings III had not been the Prosecutor.

28. Dunnings III and W-6 engaged in commercial sex at various locations, including W-6's home in a Lansing trailer park, the Fairfield Hotel and the Causeway Bay Hotel in Lansing.

29. W-6 had never engaged in prostitution before the proposition by, and resulting commercial sex with, Dunnings III. Likewise, she has not had commercial sex with any other person after being induced to engage in prostitution by Dunnings III."[116] *(Text bolded by Author)* *

With these charges, at the exact same time he lets Larry Nassar off for his sexual harassment charges, Dunnings is involved in a violent trafficking ring himself. He was facing 14 charges and over 20 years for a laundry list of offenses.[117] **He took a plea deal** and ended up being charged with one felony and one misdemeanor which boiled it down and he faced only (up to) 6 years in prison.[118] **He skated away with one year in county jail and three years' probation.[119]** And instead of facing the very criminals he threw in jail in the county in which he practiced, Sheriff Wriggelsworth, the same Sheriff that was involved in catching him (see previous comments from **Sheriff Wriggelsworth), decided to place him in Clinton County jail where he served one year and three years' probation.[120]**

His charge was **"misconduct in office and using the services of a prostitute."[121]** The article is quoted as saying, " The defense attorney argued that another jail other than the Ingham County jail should be sought."[122] and, "Prior to the sentencing the defense argued Dunnings is a sex addict who had sought treatment after his arrest and his addiction should factor into the sentence."[123] **Dunnings broke down and quoted Bible verses** while addressing the court prior to the sentencing. **He** admitted to the court that "I betrayed the trust of the people."[124] "Dunnings apologized to his family and community. The former prosecutor explained he had been sexually abused as a child. The judge acknowledged that the defense had submitted approximately 40 letters of support for Dunnings."[125]

The document adds, "He served as Ingham County's Prosecutor for decades, prosecuting human trafficking cases and speaking out against the illegal industry which is heavily connected to prostitution."[126]

As we can see, these incidences are not happenstance. They cover up the ring, and it's more than a perverted judge looking for a hooker to sleep with. Propaganda made sure to mention he was a "victim of sexual abuse" and acknowledged that the defense had submitted approximately 40 letters of support for Dunnings."[127] In a telling last comment, the article reminds us that he prosecuted human trafficking.[128] As it goes, years of more abuse from Nassar proceeded as a direct result of Dunning's deliberate negligence (at best); he can't excuse his decisions in the Nassar case for lack of information. Dunning's and Attorney General Bill Schuette had come out strong against sex trafficking, placing him in the forefront of the up-to-date news and education on the subject.[129]

Let's continue the Michigan State case.

As we left off, Nassar was becoming unveiled. The case reopened from 2014 where a woman reported to both police and MSU that Larry Nassar sexually assaulted her (**an allegation the university deemed unfounded**); during the appointment, Doctor Nassar "cupped her buttocks, massaged her breast and vaginal area and attempted to insert his finger into her vagina."[130] A month after she reported to the MSU's internal **Title IX Investigator,** and the media reported on the story with the following comments:

> "She shared her story with the State Journal last year and
> said there were two facts **she reported to an investigator
> that weren't included in the final report.** The woman

said Nassar was sexually aroused while he was touching her and, despite her requests that he stop, he didn't stop touching her until she physically removed his hands from her body.". . . "Three months after **the university opened an internal investigation, it cleared Nassar of any violations of MSU's sexual assault and harassment policy** and said that the woman didn't understand the 'nuanced' difference between sexual assault and an appropriate medical procedure."[131]

The article goes on to say, "After the university cleared Nassar in 2014, he and **William Stampel, the dean of MSU's College of Osteopathic Medicine** where Nassar worked, reached an agreement on new protocols Nassar would be required to abide by, including wearing gloves and having someone else in the room during examinations. That agreement, as outlined in an email, didn't include a follow-up mechanism to ensure Nassar was compliant."[132]

To conclude that Larry didn't violate these women and was following proper medical procedure, Michigan State used **four experts in the medical field that were employed by MSU and were closely linked to Doctor Nassar, including someone Nassar himself recommended to the investigator.**[133] One of them, **Dr. Brooke Lemmen**, stepped down from her position in January of 2017.[134] Before she resigned, Dr. Lemmen had removed confidential patient files from the university.[135] **She reported that Dr. Larry Nassar had requested them however said she didn't give them to him, but returned them to Michigan State instead.**[136]

That report, as you can see, makes entirely no sense—Dr. Nassar requested she remove confidential patient files, she did and then did a U-turn and returned them to Michigan State? Why did she take them out to begin with?

Following the original report in 2014, the **police department at Michigan State** investigated the criminal allegations from the woman and once a report was made, sent its findings to **Ingham County Prosecuting Attorney's Office** for review.[137] Stuart Dunnings III didn't charge Nassar, and the **MSU Chief of Police Jim Dunlap** was quoted as said that "when prosecutors told his department they weren't issuing charges, they said that what Nassar did might be a legitimate medical procedure."[138] This was quoted in a press conference.[139]

The Police Chief is on record as saying that after their investigation, this sexual crime passes as a medical procedure.[140] We can conclude then, either they are covering up, or his IQ is so very low, he is inept to do his job. Also, it was reported to the police that Nassar was sexually aroused during their medical appointments.[141] Law enforcement covered it up, and failed beyond just an accident. Too many women were saying the same thing, and too many reports were coming in over and over reporting the same thing. It makes you wonder **why anyone would cover it up over and over? To what gain?** There's only one answer: There is a larger system at play here. Let's continue the story to see the system and its working parts.

MSU AND THE WEB OF THE RING

Nassar was accused again and charged with the same crime in July of 2015 with the same charges to the same people that handled the last case.[142] On July 1, the **MSU police department-the same department that was mentioned in the last case** that shut down allegations— submitted a warrant request for a fourth-degree criminal sexual conduct charge.[143] In Michigan, that's considered a misdemeanor.[144] Five and a half months later, in December of 2015, **prosecutors denied the charges commending Larry Nassar** and calling his medical disguise of sexual assault to be "a very innovative and helpful manipulation."[145]

Interjecting a question: how would police officers be able to determine what is suited for medical practice?

The Captain of the police, Valerie O'Brien (who was working as a detective at the time) stated in a report, "Nassar stated he purposely touched her there. Nassar stated he has been doing this since 1997. 'What now, what happened?'"[146] The article then reports, "She later emailed **Assistant Prosecutor Steve Kwasnik, who denied the warrant,** and said she agreed with the decision, that it appeared Nassar and Thomashow told similar versions of the events, and that Nassar appeared to be telling the truth during his interview."[147] **Prosecutors denied charges three times, MSU Police Chief Jim Dunlap said,** with the first two being verbal and the final in an email.[148] The same Police Chief that was fully aware of the charges brought against the same predator. That investigation was a massive debacle. **The question still remains: to what gain are all of these professional people covering for? Why protect a man that is blatantly sexually assaulting women and children?** Adding insult to injury, the final **Title IX report was written by the investigator, Kristine Moore, from MSU.**[149] She wrote **two different versions of the report and gave one to the victim and another to Larry Nassar and his higher-up, Doctor William Strampel.**[150] The "substantive text in the conclusion section" that wasn't added in the report to the **victim's version was not released by Michigan State University.**[151]

All of the allegations that proceeded landed in the lap of the University that attempted a cover-up too big to cover up. **The MSU athletic department** got involved with what looked like a last ditch effort to put a bandage on the inevitable explosion. With constant allegations that Doctor Larry Nassar was digitally penetrating patients without gloves, being sexually aroused during medical visits, grabbing women inappropriately, and more and more women coming forward, the Athletic Department panicked. As the news came out that he'd been **indicted on federal child pornography charges,** he was found with over **37,000 child**

porn files including videos of himself he'd recorded with his GoPro camera as he groomed children whose normal was forever changed.[152]

This poses several questions. **1. What is the threshold in law where we go from, "He just is a perverted sick pedophile who watches child pornography" to, "He's producing child pornography with intent to distribute?" That hasn't been considered in the legal system because they're either part of the trafficking system or they're not aware that it works that way**. If this were a drug, the law is different with different penalties if caught with (for example) marijuana. If someone is caught with x amount, they get a possession charge.[153] The consequences are far less than the felony charge of "possession with intent to distribute."[154] As a society, we need to examine this and realize that Nassar, not having a "type" (which most pedophiles do) in which he was violating (i.e. boys, girls with blonde hair, etc.)—perpetrators go after a certain type of victim. If it's free ranging with no rhyme or reason, it's a sign of grooming for trafficking.[155,156]

As the story leaked, the **gymnastics team members were told to keep quiet by coaches and Athletic Department faculty**. An emergency meeting was held with the **team meeting in September.[157] The report reads as follows:**

"The gymnastics team was a called into a meeting [in September 2016...]" says the woman's lawyer, Jamie White. "And a representative from the university came to talk to the girls, informed them that Mr. Nassar was under investigation, and went on to tell them that **they were not to speak with anybody about this, including the media, their families, the authorities, and so on.**

One victim's attorney said **she didn't recognize the school official who told the team, in September 2016, not to answers questions from reporters or police. Instead, White says, they were told to refer all questions to the MSU legal department.** The victim's attorney stated, "And what's particular about our client, is **they did a**

follow up with her. And told her, **her cell phone could be subject to checks.** And she interpreted that as being, you know, in the event that she was to talk to someone, they might find out about it. **And she was quite intimidated** by that, especially in light of the fact that she was a victim." The university spokesperson **Jason Cody declined to say whether MSU was investigating whether any staff members discouraged students from talking to police.**

"It is not appropriate to offer comment on ongoing litigation, especially on matters that may be subject of an ongoing criminal investigation or internal review," Cody said in an email Wednesday. **"What I can tell you is MSU Police are investigating all allegations thoroughly. If evidence is uncovered that an MSU employee sought to interfere with the criminal case or prevent individuals from coming forward, we will take appropriate action. The university will not tolerate any interference with the investigation."[158]** *(Text bolded by Author)*

The entire cover up IS interference with the investigation.

As with any quick cover from the higher ups, fall-men (and women) have to take the fall. Loyalty comes into play here, and the lowest on the totem pole gets the bad rap. The first to have to take one for the ring was women's gymnastics Head Coach Kathie Klages. She announced her retirement one day after being suspended by MSU.[159]

Two women say they told Klages about Nassar's alleged abuse back in the 1990's, but claim she **downplayed their concerns and told them they "misunderstood"** legitimate medical practices.[160] Loyalty remained her currency as she released a statement that Klages' was "deeply disturbed" by the allegations against Nassar.[161] "Had she ever received any information to cast doubt on the appropriateness of that trust in Dr. Nassar, she would have reacted immediately to protect her gymnasts."[162]

The next up to bat was the coach's boss, **Athletic Director Mark Hollis.** Hollis said that Klages' suspension was related to "allegations that members of the women's **gymnastics team were discouraged from cooperating with the ongoing law enforcement investigation** of Dr. Nassar."[163] Hollis claims the coach's "passionate defense of Dr. Nasser created an emotionally charged environment for the team."[164] But **Coach Klages wasn't the one who told the team that they shouldn't talk to police**, or that their phones might be checked, but reports stated there were two athletic department staff that attended that meeting and made those threats.[165]

The attorney reported her that client's statement was that she "didn't remember their names but gave a physical description."[166] This begs the question: is she covering her guilt because she told the athletes they shouldn't talk to police? Or is she covering her ass from getting killed because she knows if she snitches, they'll kill her. Organized crime is notorious for having you swim with the fishes. With that idea, it was reported that Klages told a mother of one of the athletes that the child pornography may have been "planted."[167]

"'Coach Klages told her in no uncertain terms that **her daughter was misreading what had occurred.** And what had occurred to her was legitimate medical treatment … and my client's mother said, 'Well what about the child pornography? Doesn't that give you some alarm?' And Coach Klages went on to tell her that she thought the **child pornography had been planted, potentially, by someone who had some other interest in a lawsuit or something.** Coach Klages then went on to say, 'I would trust this man with my daughters and my granddaughters.' Klages' attorney did not return multiple requests for comment."[168]

After reading the article of this cover up, we now see reports of Nassar's sexual abuse by at least 265 women and underage girls.[169] **All the while, the school was creating a massive illusion to avoid exposure that involved law enforcement, politicians, lawyers, coaches, Title IX** directors, parents, board members of the gymnastics club, collegiate and elite-level gymnasts, the USA Gymnastics organization, medical professionals, administrators, college staff, educational departments, fans, and a plethora of other citizens whom he groomed at best and paid off at worst. The end game is money. They aided and abetted this criminal act of mass producing traumatized women to further the agenda of one of the biggest financial structures that holds up the economy.

Let's keep digging.

TITLE IX: THE SHOT-FAKE

During this atrocity of abuse and rape, the MSU athletic department was having another scandal on their hands. Their basketball and football teams were being heavily accused of sexual misconduct which added into the same system of the coverup.[170] Top players were frequently reported for sexual violence and many of the cases reported being victims of the team's gang rape—an athletic cultural norm where teammates rape the same woman in as a sign of team bonding.[171] As women came forward with horrific stories, the same threats continued; the women were blamed and forced not to tell.[172]

In a report from ESPN, **Michigan State Basketball Program and the Football Program have both been reported as having massive cover-ups for their players.**[173] On August 29, 2010 a female student went with two basketball stars to their dorm room, when two basketball stars proceeded to rape her on the floor of their dorm room.[174] After they finished raping her, she left and called her friend who went with her.[175] Two days later when she made the police report.[176]

When the police report was requested, the players' names were anonymous; a blacked out line on a police report covered the names.[177] The survivor of this crime, Carolyn Shaner, reported that the **police assured her they'd call the district attorney and recommend it be handled as the highest form of sexual assault.**[178] When she was questioned by **the prosecutor** however, she was told, **"You're accusing MSU basketball team of this. You're going to have to be a lot stronger than you are. If you can't handle me you won't be able to handle a jury."**[179] Because she was emotionally upset and didn't appear to be able to "handle" the questioning, they decided it was insufficient testimony and couldn't move forward.[180] Debra Martinez, **who was the assistant District Attorney at the time, now is employed in the Title IX office at Michigan State University.**[181]

Two days after her report, school officials moved the two athletes into different housing, and under federal law, they were mandated to do an investigation.[182] **An outside attorney was brought in, and when questioning the victim, it was the same slut shaming script we've all heard of with questions like, "Why'd you go there? . . .Why'd you go hang out, etc.?"**[183] **The attorney decided the athletes didn't violate policy and dropped the case entirely.**[184] The basketball coach, Tom Izzo, did nothing to punish the players, and they were able to be the stars of the show; they celebrated both on campus and nationally as they sold out stadiums and brought the university big dollars.

In 2010 there were **two more reports of the same team under the same coaching staff.**[185] The male athlete was reported during the MSU's trip to the Final Four, **of punching a female in the face at a bar and he suffered no consequences** in 2010 when he sat with Coach Izzo and continued his career as a student assistant coach.[186] Despite his pending criminal charges, **Coach Izzo and the Michigan State athletic department** allowed him to continue coaching.[187] Just a few months later, **Coach Izzo signed a new contract and the same President that turned a blind eye to the reports of Larry Nassar endorsed coach Izzo and the basketball team and even included a new contract.**[188] But the basketball cover-up wasn't over.

Later that summer, **another woman reported being gang raped by three Michigan State basketball players along with other men.**[189]

The Athletic Director was informed directly of the allegations including the names; **the victim reported it directly to the Athletic Department**.[190] This was the first reported to anyone; there were others that hadn't had the courage to speak up and for obvious reasons.

The Athletic Director told the victims' parents he'd conduct his own investigation personally assuring them it would be handled.[191] But after it was discussed with the basketball team, **no players were reprimanded and** this case wasn't reported to anyone outside of the athletic department.[192] When questioned, one of the perpetrators denied hitting any woman and "doesn't recall" raping anyone.[193] Ironically, **school officials wouldn't comment**.[194]

By June of 2011, the victim was dissatisfied with how it was handled.[195] She filed a Title IX compliant with the United States Educational Department.[196] Betsy DeVos, who sits as the Secretary of Education (appointed by President Donald Trump) is from Michigan.[197] They reported back and didn't find anything wrong with MSU's findings, but did agree that the Federal Investigators erred in the delay of the investigation.[198] As **investigators were then sent to Michigan State** to comb through policy and procedure, they spent hours asking staff and students questions.[199] What they found across the board was that the **MSU athletes have a reputation of engaging in sexual assault and harassment.**[200] While the investigation was ongoing, **the school coincidentally didn't give federal investigators any records on Nassar,** even though they had them.[201] The **school officials said "it was an unfortunate oversight."**[202] ESPN reporter said, "They have actively suppressed the files on reports on sexual assault and the efforts to hide them have **a lot of people wondering what's behind the curtain?**"[203]
But before we answer the obvious, let's not forget about the Michigan State football program.

In June of 2017, **Michigan State was also addressing sexual assault allegations on four football players; twelve more reports have been** issued since the football coach was hired, six of which were reports of gang rape.[204]

In October of 2007, a woman was drinking and playing cards with **football player**s, and once intoxicated, she was taken to a hotel, and **violently gang raped**.[205] She dropped out of school and had irreconcilable mental health issues from complex PTSD.[206] Her mother in an interview with ESPN, stated she would hear her screaming in her sleep and calling out the players by name, and would fight them off of her.[207] **In November of 2012 at the age of 26, she died as a result of an overdose.**[208] Shortly after her death, her parents found her writings in the trunk of her car giving an account of **what happened to her at the hands of the football team.**[209] Her mother took her notebook to MSU campus police, and when questioned, one of the alleged rapists denied any involvement, but **gave insight into locker room talk and how common the conversation was had about running trains on women.**[210] **He said "they talked in code. They have different names for different girls."**[211] **According to campus police report, the football players listed in the journal denied knowing her, so they closed the case.**[212]

In the first four months of 2017, **four football players were reported for forcing a woman to have oral sex**, and as expected, MSU denied request to do interview.[213]

TRUE STORY

In 1997, late at night on a weekday, the local strip club was empty of customers and the dancers were getting ready to close up shop. With only thirty minutes left to go, they sat around and talked a bit and got ready to pay out and head home. Suddenly the manager came to the back dressing room to announce that the **Michigan State football team bus** had just pulled up and they were going to have to stay longer for work. Instead of closing at two a.m., they'd stay open until at least three a.m. As the room filled with linebackers and running backs, Amber took stage at a peak prize fighting weight of 120 lbs. The entire room erupted with testosterone and the normal five-minute stage set doubled in time for every football player to make sure he got his money's worth tipping the naked dancer. The couches were full, the money was flying and the pockets of the working girls doubled within ninety minutes. Everyone went home happy. And because **payout was 40% to the club,** even though each dancer was independently contracted as a 1099 employee, the illegal payout ensured the club's manager had a pleasing look on his face.

Here are the questions you should be having:

1. Who paid for the team bus?

2. Where'd the student athletes get the cash to buy hours' worth of $20 lap dances that only lasted two minutes at a time, and throw $1 bills on stage at every proceeding act after Amber?

3. Why are they on a misogynistic college sponsored field trip on a weekday?

Most importantly though, where's the money coming from?

4. Could that be the incentive of the entire cover up?

The more the athletes are satisfied, the more money the school makes. But on the surface, that's not reason enough to put your entire school at risk over one pervert that likes to fondle gymnasts. That doesn't add up. Surely there's more than meets the eye; more dollars to pay people off to keep everyone out of trouble. When you step back, you see the same ring that happens in poverty neighborhoods goes all the way up and Benjamin Franklin gets a lot bigger. Money is the name of the game and women are owned and bought and sold to feed the pockets of the higher-ups that sit all the way up. Sex slaves are being mass produced in the same department as the groomed predators, and everyone goes home with secret wads of cash in their pockets. Either look the other way, or help the system stay by covering up the insidious sex for sale by using your vocational position.

As we see, Title IX directors are the perfect cover. With billions and possibly trillions of dollars at hand, that position is appointed by **traffickers posing as coaches, athletic directors, and presidents of universities . . . and they're linked to politicians, judges, educators, doctors, attorneys, accountants, media reporters, pastors, law enforcement, and every other profession that covers up the sale of people. They pay off attorneys and law enforcement and/or "convince" them not to ask questions and look the other way.**
The wolves are everywhere in sheep's clothing and they've infiltrated every social system within the mainstream.

Many have heard that trafficking is "right in our own backyard." And it is. More than you'd expect. **This stands as one of the economic pillars in the "Land of the Free".** And the same way the victims are silenced, when dealing with organized crime, the women aren't the only ones being pimped. Hush money pays. And the power is in the dollar bill. There is too much at stake for silence not to be used on the victims or anyone who poses a threat of exposure. Per the law's definition, they use "force, fraud or coercion" to ensure that they get to hide in the shadows.[214] As the data proves, it's the ones you least expect.
Let's take a look at another example where Title IX was used as the cover as was other positions to hide a sex scandal in college sports.

BAYLOR U AND THE REGENTS

The scandal at Baylor University started as stories leaked in September of 2003. A new athletic director was hired to come in and "clean up the program" after a basketball player shot and killed his teammate.[215] The basketball coach was caught on tape trying to cover the scandal and was caught trying to pitch the lie that the deceased player was a drug dealer, causing an illusion that he was involved in dangerous behavior leading to his death.[216] News broke the story that head coach David Bliss was fired, and with the new athletic director Tom Stanton on board, the media reported that the house was being cleaned.[217] In 2007, a new football coach, Art Briles was brought in.[218] And in 2010, a new president, Ken Starr was hired.[219]

Ken Starr was an interesting choice in hindsight; he was the Independent Counsel who gave the investigative account of the sex scandal in the White House with Monica Lewinsky when Bill Clinton was in office in 1998.[220] Furthermore, just three years after he took the position, President Starr and his wife Alice campaigned for a Virginia school administrator who was a convicted pedophile who'd admitted to molesting five children under the age of fourteen.[221] The judge in his case decided that, rather than allow him to work for Mr. Starr, a forty-three year prison sentence was a better fit for his future.[222] The President and his wife were advocating for him to receive community service instead, however their efforts failed. This begs the question—why would someone in his position, with access to young women and a prominent figure in the community, with cover ups on sexual abuse cases already on his plate— make such an effort to rid a convicted pedophile of charges and hire him at his university?

As the story goes, the President's efforts to hire a pedophile (combined with the plethora of reported sexual assaults on campus) simultaneously accompanied the new faces of new staff. His attempts to produce yet another disguise for the breeding ground of sexual violence was starting to ooze. Mass amounts of sexual violence were reported in a short period of time. Given that only a fraction of sex crimes are reported, the ones that are reported are covered up and dismissed. In one study, 83% of women do not report when they've been a victim of rape or sexual assault.[223] Therefore, this data is not a reflection of reality concerning how many women were victimized, but only approximately 17% of the real sum total.

The reports of violence against women accumulated quickly and word got out that Baylor wasn't as "cleaned up" as they portrayed to be.

Scandal after scandal of football athletes gang raping, beating, sexually assaulting, harassing and stalking women on campus were reported.[224] There were rumors of maltreatment from the faculty and staff all the way up to the President of the University, and as such, the school was once again under scrutiny.[225] In 2014, after finally being forced by the Department of Education, Baylor hired its first Title IX Coordinator, Patty Crawford.[226] To say Ms. Crawford put a bandage on a tumor would be an understatement. Upon further examination, Ms. Crawford may've had more motive than just reporting incidents; in other words, covering up these incidents seemed more evident as time went on, and her incentive was blatant.[22]

PATTY CAKE

Following her departure from Baylor U, Patty Crawford disclosed to the media that hundreds of sexual misconduct charges were being reported by female students, yet dismissed by higher ups during her tenure as Title IX Director at Baylor.[228] Two years into her position, her salary was just over $1,000,000 and included three pay raises, a $12,000 office renovation expansion, and a three-day spa retreat funded by the university.[229] In the middle of the crisis, she requested her salary increase to $2,000,000 but it was denied.[230] Reports say she quit her job because she was "set up to fail" in the role and was prohibited from doing her job.[231] In one report, the administrator and coaches responded to the mass amount of incoming confessions from victims by stating that it would be "great" if police kept quiet from questioning the women.[232]

Please also be reminded; the average salary of a Title IX Coordinator is $46,639.[233] That's an interesting pay gap between the average salary and Ms. Crawford's salary.

As the story progressed into 2017, a huge cover-up was unraveling. It seemed at first that Baylor's Title IX office was attempting to hide things that the University had failed to deal with, such as the many gang rapes by the football team.[234] This is commonly considered "team bonding" across the domestic athletic scene, and is "normal" in the Division 1 college football and men's basketball subculture. It's common knowledge and openly discussed in Division 1 locker rooms across the country—almost like a rite of passage.

We can assume then, that if this is culturally acceptable behavior across the board, the possibility exists that Baylor athletics and administration was also hiding several other criminal activities that were prevalent throughout the team. Let's not dismiss the school administration was recorded as telling a victim raped by a football player that, even though she had a No Contact Order in place against her violator, after he called her a slut on several different occasions as well as a whore on several other occasions, the school still deemed it as consensual sex and after reporting the violations of the No Contact Order, she contacted the Title IX office to report the violation, and the victim was told to "go out another door" when leaving class to avoid further contact.[235] The rape victim had to adjust because no one was protecting her Civil Rights. We could also assume then, that this were running rampant on the school campus, and extremely concentrated within the football program.

Could it be, however, that even after they cleaned house yet again, including the University President, the Title IX Director and the Coaches of the alleged guilty sports, that there's still something that needs to be hidden and protected? It certainly isn't the victims. If it was just malpractice in the name of reputation and the love of the sport, then why not come out with the reports of Pepper Hamilton LLP that was hired on September 2, 2015? The Philadelphia-based law firm was hired to conduct an independent external investigation into how the university handles cases of alleged sexual violence.[236]

THE REGENTS

In December 2016, the University's *Regents* (governing board of a college) received a comprehensive briefing from Pepper Hamilton's reports.[237] The briefing took place after Pepper Hamilton uncovered an underreported and overly realistic amount of arrests because of rapes by football players, fraternity presidents, and more mishandled sexual misconduct (including reports that President Starr actually was informed specifically of some these events).[238]

The Regents that received the report decided not to release them to the public and even went the extra mile and barred two Tribune-Herald Reporters from attending their meeting.[239] Ironically enough, the building where the meeting transpired was the Baylor Research and Innovation Collaborative, which received public funds for its renovation in recent years, including funds from McLennan County and the cities of Waco and Bellmead.[240] Using the excuse that Baylor was a private university appeared to be a smoke-and-mirrors attempt to justify why they were allowed to refrain from the reporting. Because they used public funding, this made their argument obsolete. Nevertheless, the school continued to refuse the disclosure of the Pepper Hamilton Investigation Reports.[241]

Thirteen days after *The Regents* publicly denied the comprehensive briefing, details surfaced from the report stating "Baylor University's handling of sexual assault cases were an institutional failure at every level of Baylor's administration" and it "impacted the response to individual cases and the Baylor community as a whole."[242]

Within the week, President Ken Starr decided to resign as chancellor.[243] He ironically expressed a strong desire for the full body of the Pepper Hamilton information to be released in hopes that the public would get a clear picture of how the University actually handled sexual assault allegations.[244]A day after his resignation, the Baylor Line Foundation (Formerly the Baylor Alumni Association), other alumni, and sexual assault survivors were supportive of his request for the full disclosure of Pepper Hamilton investigation reports.[245]

The Interim President, however, said the only portion of the report that can and will be released were the facts and findings; the 105 recommendations that Pepper and Hamilton had suggested.[246] He continued that the board of *Regents* and former president Ken Starr heard the briefings in the form of survivor stories.[247] His comment to the media continued that, "There is no secret report out there. This is the report, and making it public was incredibly courageous on [the *Regents'*] part,"[248] Garland said. "Frankly, that Pepper Hamilton report, you know, if you took all the case notes and redacted out names, you basically have what we have in the Pepper Hamilton report."[249] By this, we see the sheer cover-up; Baylor was not concerned about releasing the 105 recommendations, although to the public, the illusion of that was created. Baylor was instead keeping the stories of the survivors that existed inside of that report and the details of what was happening on campus.[250]

When former President Starr was questioned by the local newspaper in late September of 2016, he countered the argument that he and/or the athletic department (including the former football coach) mishandled the sexual assault investigations.[251] He continued to campaign for the full disclosure of the Pepper Hamilton investigation; legally, we know he wouldn't be allowed to state exactly why. It does lead to the assumption that something in there hidden is something he's been made aware of, and if they release it, the information would reveal who's really responsible. Further supporting this assumption, the football coach, after being fired on June 24th, 2016, had already announced he was under contractual obligation not to speak on the outside investigation of Pepper Hamilton.[252,253] Just prior, he filed a motion with his attorney "accusing Baylor's lawyers of a conflict of interest and alleging wrongful termination, saying that his firing was a "camouflage" by Baylor to "distract from its own institutional failure to comply"[254] with federal laws regarding sexual assault. There were rumors that the football coach settled with Baylor; within 24 hours he withdrew his motion.[255] Meanwhile, Title IX Coordinator Patty Crawford resigned in October and was vocal to the media about her disappointment with the restrictions placed by the University that hindered and disabled her from doing her job.[256] After public comments, the University responded by alluding to Crawford's settlement request for one million dollars and the right to retain book and movie rights.[257] The university expressed that they were "surprised at her request" and found it "troubling . . . and we can't explain her motivation."[258] Crawford's attorney said that by making those comments, Baylor may be "breaking the law."[259]

Ironically, the university also stated that "our understanding is that Patty was disappointed in her role in implementing the recommendations that resulted from the Pepper Hamilton investigation."[260] As the dust settled, two opposing teams, in an effort to either expose or protect the findings in this report, are in a messy legal battle over the contents in the Pepper Hamilton Investigation report. On one side, the University's Regents were using all the physical and intellectual resources they could to ensure the information was kept confidential. On the other side, those who'd been presented publicly as the guilty party responsible for the violation of women's Civil Rights are vocally crying out in tandem with the victims, Alumni, Donors and overall public for the release of the information.[261] Like a brilliant chess match with poker moves, Patty Crawford calls a brilliant bluff. Since she's not legally able to discuss the information concerning the topic at hand, she requests a million-dollar severance package, accompanied by book and movie rights. This places her in a win/win situation and creates a catch-22 for the Regents. By placing them in a position to either pay her more hush money and give her a piece of the cover up they've been paying her to cover up, which by she sells the rights of the movie and book to publishing companies and movie producers where they tell the story which then clears her name without her breaking the non-disclosure, or they refuse the settlement and the pressure builds for more attention as to why they're adamant concerning the content remaining a secret in the reports, she wins. Patty's attorney is under contractual obligation not to release what she knows from the university.

In an interview, Crawford reported that upper-level administrators interfered with her ability to do her job. She was quoted in the interview saying, "The harder I worked, the more resistance I received from senior leadership."[262] Ms. Crawford also posted on social media about the "cowardly and dishonest mentality of the millionaires running Baylor," and also added, "They're escalating discrimination, retaliation, trying to buy my integrity and now bullying their way through the media."[263] As the Regents continued to create the illusion that the ball was dropped by the football program, the athletic office, the administration, as a whole all the way up the president (all the while using each higher up during the process to join arms and stand as their protector as they blamed the ones underneath), their attempt to mask the responsible party started to become unraveled. It appeared that everyone below the top in the chain of commands was being paid off to look the other way, aiding and embedding in the trafficking ring while positioning themselves as traffickers as well. Hush money was received by all now former employees of the scandal by way of feeding their self-interest of money and power of their position. They legally could not disclose what they knew, however the information they knew that wasn't being presented caused their reputation to be tarnished, pride of their power being stripped, and finally breaking loyalty (although the motives for breaking loyalty are clearly impure-had they done this with the interest of the victims instead of themselves, this wouldn't be such a huge investigation), they started to point to the truth within the confines of their legal ability, assuming they'd all signed contractual nondisclosures.

In an attempt to continue the cover-up, The Regents (or whomever is behind the curtain) created their own monster. They violated one of the currencies of the culture. Loyalty remember, in this world of sex for sale and organized crime, has a high intrinsic value. By breaking loyalty to too many previous allies in an effort to cover up criminal activity, they fell on their own sword, and it backfired when those very people realized they were used as a pawn. Since loyalty was broken by the Regents, the pawns allied together, and (although guilty of receiving profit for the same crime) they were blinded by their conditioning and started to collectively fire back. In this culture, disloyalty is like stealing. So in an attempt to gain back what had been stolen, they made it clear how the system was working (i.e. I'm guilty for receiving money from this, but I'm not the one behind it, and I'm not taking the bullet for the true perpetrator who is throwing me under the bus). As the army of the "falsely accused" grew, they broke the loyalty code themselves and refused to take the bullet. The entire system started bursting at the seams and truth started to reveal itself as to "who" is behind the iron curtain. Without reference to how the system works however, the legal suit continues, and it appears as just "legal mudslinging" to the general public. Let's keep digging.

By October of 2016, Baylor continued their attempt at their insidious veil. In an attempt to divert attention from the protected document and the secrets it contained, they publicly reported that they followed the procedure recommended by Pepper Hamilton, and per the recommendations of the investigation, they created a new position for a Title IX Chief Compliance Officer to ensure it was executed more effectively.[264] They named Doug Welch—the attorney that represented the University against Former Football Coach Art Briles.[265] The problem arose when a lawsuit was filed by one of the victims who sued Coach Briles and Former Athletic Director Ian McCaw in "unspecified damages."[266] The motion that Briles retracted just before his firing lists Welch as adding information from that lawsuit which the school used

when terminating the football coach's employment with the university.[267]
In other words, Doug Welch used his power as an attorney for Art Briles
to then undermine Art Briles and side with the University to fire him.

In the same report, incriminating texts by the former coach were disclosed:

- On April 8. 2011. after a freshman defensive tackle was cited for illegal consumption of alcohol. Coach Briles sent a text message to an assistant coach: "Hopefully he's under radar enough they won't recognize name – did he get ticket from Baylor police or Waco? ... Just trying to keep him away from our judicial affairs folks...."

- On February 11. 2013. an assistant coach notified Coach Briles of a claim by a female student-athlete that a football player brandished a gun at her. Coach Briles responded: "what a fool – she reporting to authorities" The assistant coach texted back: "She's acting traumatized ... Trying to talk her calm now... Doesn't seem to want to report though." Coach Briles texted: "U gonna talk to [the player]." The assistant coach concluded: "Yes sir. just did. Caught him on the way to class... Squeezed him pretty good." The matter was never reported to Judicial Affairs.

- On September 13 2013. Shillinglaw sent a text to Coach Briles about a player who got a massage and "supposedly exposed himself and asked for favors. She [masseuse] has a lawyer but wants us to handle with discipline and counseling." Coach Briles' first response was "What kind of discipline... She a stripper?" When Shillinglaw said the player made the request at a salon and spa while getting a massage. Coach Briles wrote. "Not quite as bad."

- On September 20. 2013. after a player was arrested for assault and threatening to kill a non-athlete. a football operations staff official tried to talk the victim out of pressing criminal charges. Meanwhile. Coach Briles texted Athletics Director Ian McCaw: "Just talked to [the player] – he said Waco PD was there – said they were going to keep it quiet – Wasn't a set up deal... I'll get shill (Shillinglaw) to ck on Sibley (local attorney Jonathan Sibley)." Athletics Director Ian McCaw replied: "That would be great if they kept it quiet!"

268

The Dust has Settled: The Pepper Hamilton Report

Toward the end of 2016, The Baylor Line Foundation (aka The Baylor Alumni Association) was displeased with the Regent's decision to speak to the press about the scandal and called it "part of a carefully orchestrated public relations campaign."[269] They reminded the Regents (and the public) of their obligation to fully disclose the Pepper Hamilton Investigation, which they still refused to disclose.[270] The more they kept quiet, gave partial truths to the media and refused to show what was in the document, the more people grew restless. During this same time, Ms. Crawford did a press interview in which she was very clear about her feelings that the scandal was coming "from the top."[271] The top of what? And is Ms. Crawford aware of what 'the top' is?

Coincidentally (in reference to components in the Michigan State University scandal) more press continued when Acrobatics and Tumbling (i.e. gymnastics) Coach Laprise Williams said she'd filed the reports she'd received by her athletes of more sexual assaults by Baylor football players (and other men on campus), but she was quickly told to "stick to coaching."[272]

As many of you know, the NCAA (National Collegiate Athletic Association) is the organization that oversees all collegiate sports.[273] In November 2016, (although they'd decided not to get involved with Baylor's rape debacle), they expressed that their only concern was to ensure there wasn't "preferential treatment for the athletes" by the school in regards to the discipline they were receiving for their actions.[274] The irony is, the entire scandal is over the refusal to protect the victims and the lack of discipline and accountability for the athletes. That's like saying, "We don't want to get involved with the problem. But the problem is what we're checking on." Without saying anything, the NCAA looks suspicious. By practical thinking, they've conveniently looked the other way with a public statement that contradicts itself in the hopes that no one notices. It's smoke and mirrors, and it reveals how intrinsic the wicked web spins and how many spiders take hits for black widows. With all other facts and data, while trying to convince the public of their illusionist tricks, they deliberately fumble the focus to something obsolete. But again, the question remains: to what gain?

Assumedly, an astronomical amount of money is the main motivator behind this scandal. As Baylor University's donors increased the pressure to hand over the full document from the Pepper Hamilton investigation, the Regents scrambled.[275] Once again, the Regents made an attempt to say, "Nothing to see here"; they created a website with full biographies of the people on their board, an email address for fielding any questions about the investigation, and meeting notes from their private meetings and upcoming events.[276] Still no report was disclosed. Not surprisingly, the lack of reporting produced the opposite effect of their desired goal. Clearly, this wasn't going to go away quietly in the night.

An increase in influential donors, including the Texas Governor, began to express their concern and as their collected voices started to harmonize, this larger group held a meeting with 650 people in attendance.[277] Everyone in that meeting agreed that leadership among the Regents needed shifting.[278] In response, the Regents said that disclosing meeting notes was more than enough, because they are a private university.[279] Apparently, the integrity of the athletic program outweighs the unimaginable trauma that these women have experienced.

By the end of 2016, the pressure was working, and the Regents decided to consider releasing more information.[280] Ironically in the same statement, they reported that Baylor was in good shape financially.[281] Unless this was a battle of nondisclosure of information surrounded by finances, those two statements and considerations seem to be contradicting, distracting and non-related. Upon further thought, they are hand in hand.

The Regents manipulated the perspective of the general public by purposefully picking and choosing which statements from the Investigation would be made public. They released a few statements that, without the full story, allude to the assumption that the guilty party were the ones they'd already fired. When these are the ONLY statements released, it appears as such. However, keep in mind that those same people are calling for a FULL disclosure of the Pepper Hamilton Investigation Report.[282] What then, are they hiding?

The fragmented report they chose to release is as follows

> ". . .In addition, the investigations were conducted in the context of a broader culture and **belief by many administrators that sexual violence "doesn't happen here."** Administrators engaged in conduct that could be perceived as **victim-blaming, focusing on the complainant's choices and actions, rather than robustly investigating the allegations, including the actions of the respondent.** In many instances, student conduct investigators conducted cursory investigations and **failed to identify and interview readily apparent witnesses or gather relevant evidence.** Student conduct investigators also applied **the preponderance of the evidence standard of proof in an inconsistent manner,** and in many instances, required a far greater level of proof than preponderance. **A lack of clearly identified reporting mechanisms, combined with insufficient training and attention to sexual and gender-based harassment and violence and other forms of interpersonal violence**, may have led to **significant underreporting by students and missed opportunities by administrators** to respond appropriately to reports.
>
> ***(Text bolded by Author)***

In Regards to the Football Program:

"In addition, some **football coaches and staff took improper steps in response to disclosures of sexual assault or dating violence** that **precluded the University from fulfilling its legal obligations. Football staff conducted their own untrained internal inquiries, outside of policy,** which improperly **discredited complainants** and **denied them the right to a fair, impartial and informed investigation,** interim measures or processes promised under University policy. In some cases, **internal steps gave the illusion of responsiveness** to complainants but **failed to provide a meaningful institutional response under Title IX.** Further, because **reports were not shared outside of athletics, the University missed critical opportunities to impose appropriate disciplinary action that would have removed offenders** from campus and possibly precluded future acts of sexual violence against Baylor students. **In some instances, the football program dismissed players for unspecified team violations and assisted them in transferring to other schools.** As a result, **some football coaches and staff abdicated responsibilities under Title IX and Clery; to student welfare; to the health and safety of complainants; and to Baylor's institutional values.**"[283,284]

(Text bolded by Author)

Although the Regents were finally forthcoming with tidbits of the report, they voted unanimously, when it was suggested by those requesting the entire report, that they did not want another outside investigation into the school's scandal.[285] They concluded and communicated that they were confident in Pepper Hamilton's findings.[286] The Regents were working with the thirteen pages of their review that had been publicly released.[287] (Please remember, the entire Pepper Hamilton Investigation was much larger than a fifteen-page document. The thirteen of fifteen pages released was only on their recommendations—not the findings in their investigation).[288] This vote came when donors from the university requested further information and gave them an option for a second opinion.[289] The Regent's board was then put up for vote, and a full investigation was requested by an organization called the Bears for Leadership Reform.[290] Baylor was expected to do the external investigation by the beginning of 2017, all the while the former football coach Art Briles filed a lawsuit against three of the Regents members.[291] The charges included libel, slander and conspiracy.[292] Baylor Regents and administrators said that "all of his proposed accusations in the lawsuit against them are false."[293]

Financial forecasts were reported, shedding light to how expensive the scandal had become; the estimated low end figure of $233 million caught more attention and heated up the pressure on the Regents.[294] If $233 million was the lower estimated amount spent on this massive cover up, imagine the amount they're covering up. The report and figures are as follows:

"On December 13, 2016, Bears for Leadership Reform, a group of notable Baylor donors, says the scandal could cost the school at least $223 million, according to a financial analysis commissioned by the group. It says Baylor has spent or will spend almost $33 million in legal, consulting and public relations costs, $30 million in fines and sanctions and more than $24 million in settlements with employees. Other costs of investigations, victim settlements, hiring new employees and Title IX compliance bring the total to $121.7 million. Also projected is $101.3 million in lost private contributions through 2019.[295] Also Tuesday, Tom Hill, an athletics employee who was fired amid the scandal, sues the Pepper Hamilton law firm. Hill claims the attorneys did not obtain pertinent facts, interviews with important witnesses, nor did they perform their duties objectively and accuses partners Gina Maisto Smith and Leslie M. Gomez of negligence and defamation."[296]

Shortly after, Pepper Hamilton law firm answered back "denying all allegations."[297]

Just when you thought all of the bombs were dropped on how many women were sexually victimized, further allegations of sexual assault were still coming in. A graduate of Baylor filed a lawsuit accusing the University of creating a culture of sexual violence where over fifty rapes in the four years she attended existed.[298] She was one of the victims of rape from the football team's "team bonding" where trains were ran. To "run a train" in this context means that a group of men wait to have sex with one girl. Usually it does not qualify as a train unless there are more than seven men involved but the term train is used to describe any number that is more than one with a female.[299] She also mentioned coaches in her lawsuit, namely Briles' son Kendal who arranged for recruits to have sex with women off campus during recruiting visits.[300] Other lawsuits continued with allegations that they conspired to keep criminal activity of the athletes out of the media and hidden from the public, including the university police department.[301] They were above the law and any and all forms of corruption including drugs, rape, assault, weapons and cheating in class were erased from the football team's records.[302]

With these further university embarrassments, the Big 12 Conference Board of Directors decided to hold back a noticeable portion of the school's revenue until they could prove that the school had changed their policy and procedures in athletics in accordance with Title IX.[303]

In a scurry of an attempt to make adjustments now that money was pulled from the school, the Regents became more forthcoming with their new website listing their members' biographies, governance documents and the future topics of their next meetings.[304] An email was even provided in an attempt to be accessible.[305]

Justice fighters and those demanding the reports called on law enforcement to ensure a massive investigation on the largest attempt at a scandal cover up the country had seen to date in history.[306] The Texas Rangers were one of the enforcement agencies called in to further the investigations.[307] Furthermore, Texas lawmakers were inspired by the discrepancy and obvious criminal activity and used their position to problem-solve by writing a bill that required third-party witnesses of testimony or event to mandatorily report sex crimes on campus.[308] The lack of reporting could result in criminal charges.[309] The intention behind it was to make it easier for victims to report without the fear of intimidation.[310] Another proposed bill would blackball sex offenders from living on college campuses.[311]

Simultaneously the college's rotted fruit still remained. Baylor settled out of court with a woman who called the school "a hunting ground for sexual predators" and reported being drugged at "the rugby house" party and abducted and raped on February 28, 2015.[312] The amount the school paid her was not public information.[313] After the settlement, five more suits are still pending against a pastor and student of their theological seminary who was arrested for sexually assaulting a child in his car.[314] Although the attempt to make accountability a mandatory structure, as long as the culture of the school fosters sexual violence toward women, nothing will change. In a culture where lawsuits have impending accusations that their football recruits were enticed to sign with their program by using "female student hostesses expected to have sex with them,"[315] it's clear that the culture needs more than just bills and laws and new staff. Something deeper is happening behind the curtain.

As these court cases of violence against women in a rape culture continued, the cover-up continued. In a telling news story, one of the Regent members was exposed in an email he'd sent to a faculty advisor referring to female students he suspected of drinking alcohol as "'perverted little tarts,' 'very bad apples,' 'insidious and inbred' and 'the vilest and most despicable of girls.'"[316] Ten alleged sexual assault victims suing Baylor attached the emails to show a culture "using the alcohol policy as a pretext to shame, silence and threaten to expel a female student."[317] This was a crippling report for them; slut shaming at a time like this is a blow they couldn't afford. It adds to the presumed explanation as to why the Pepper Hamilton Investigation Report was something they were clutching—documents that bring survivor testimony to the forefront which would prove incriminating evidence and expose the entire system of the trafficking ring. Their efforts to protect those stories were relentless, but more pressure was coming from other outside sources.

IT'S NOT OVER: THE COVER UP CONTINUES

US District Court Judge Robert Pitman ruled against the school on July 26, 2017 when he ordered them to produce the original documents in the Pepper Hamilton investigation of sexual violence and harassment from the entire records dating back to 2003 in place of the thirteen-page summary they'd given forth to date.[318] In Judge Pitman's ruling, he gave Baylor the right to withhold and disregarded all other legal systems, including the Texas Rangers, Big 12, and NCAA (the other organizations pursuing their own investigations) and dismissed their requests from disclosing the documents putting Judge Pitman the only legal enforcer to have access.[319] He did however want the inclusion of the text messages of the regent member calling women "perverted little tarts," etc. and considered it relevant to the decision he'd make in the case.[320] At this point of the investigation, the question arises—should we be concerned that Mr. Pitman is now the ONLY one who will then obtain the Pepper Hamilton Investigation Reports? The secrecy and inclusivity of the documents are what caused the alarm and protection of insidiousness to begin with.

An attorney blew the whistle when he reported that regardless of the Judge's request, they withheld parts of the documents that were ordered.[321] With proof that pages were missing, the Judge gave warning.[322] This is extremely concerning that the US District Court Judge would issue 'just a warning.'

What's even more concerning is the date required to comply with the Court's ruling of full disclosure (including all documents including notes, recordings, evidence and the notorious Pepper Hamilton investigation).[323] The trial is set for October 2018.[324]

Rah, Rah, Shish Kum Bah

While men's sports are being investigated for a long list of heinous sex crimes and other criminal behavior, and we've seen the massive scandal involving professionals using their positions to create the system (by either being the cover itself or turning a blind eye—the "good ol' boy system"), another story exposing a women's athletic team surfaced in 2017.[325] According to reports, an entire cheer team at Coastal Carolina University was investigated for an anonymous tip that lead to the uncovering of more sex for sale.[326] Cheerleaders on CCU's squad were involved in prostitution and were accused of other infractions including "paying other students to do their homework, buying alcohol for minors, and performing sex acts for financial gain" and a "long list of things."[327,328]The tip came in on March 7, 2017 directly to the President of the University, David DeCenzo.[329] He met with a few of the athletes for questioning, and investigations with the university police followed.[330] Their phones were searched, and they were dismissed from further questioning and declared innocent of the accusations.[331] The school, however, suspended their upcoming competitive cheer competition, and parents and supporters of the athletes were quoted on social media with dismay and unfair treatment from the school for no valid reason.[332] Further reports came in, however, that the allegations may not just be rumors proving the public dismay from their families and fans may have been premature, as the investigation progressed.[333] [334]

Eleven teammates not working for the escort service or strip club were aware of the other athletes' occupations due to evidence that was found when phones were searched and conversations among squad members were encouraging those involved to quit working at the strip club until after the competition so the team wouldn't be suspended.[335]

Apparently, their warning came too late; they were prohibited from going due to the investigation. [336]

When the media obtained documents from the Freedom of Information Act, they confirmed that the allegations were true.[337] Student athletes from the cheerleading team were working on websites that promoted younger women escorting for older men and their pay ranged from $100 to $1,500 per appointment with a customer, and other gifts including name-brand shoes, clothes and purses were received for their services as well.[338]

Further reports of hazing on the team were mentioned in the original anonymous letter from a "concerned parent" who thinks it is morally wrong for women to pay off people to do their work and engage in sex for sale transactions while others had to work hard for their money and their grades.[339] According to the report, the "concerned anonymous parent" was a father identified as a "heavy-set man with salt and pepper-colored hair."[340] The report reads, "The letter alleged the cheerleaders were engaged in prostitution, stripping, drinking and forcing younger cheerleaders to partake in underage drinking" and "they were not 'accepted' into the team unless they took part."[341]

Ironically, at the end of the article after the full team suspension, an attorney for the girls, Amy Lawrence was quoted saying,

> "Would this ever happen to a Male Sports Team? We have all read
> about male athletes at Coastal Carolina being accused of drugs,
> domestic violence and rape," *Lawrence's statement concluded,*
> "Yet, most of those men are still playing the sport and not one team
> was suspended in retribution for the actual crimes of their
> teammates."[342]

The obvious question is, why did this comment go uninvestigated? Clearly, this is the cultural double standard: a rape culture that fosters the exploitation of female sexuality, and—when exposed—the consequences, punishment, and actions by the school are vastly different than the responses we're finding in male sports. Is the only factor that differentiates the amount of attention professionals decide to give these cases that determines how much time and money spent simply just the variant of gender? Given, and rhetorically speaking, yes. But there's an underlying issue again illustrated in this example. Women's cheerleading doesn't make the college any money. Men's football and basketball, however, are big business with a lot at stake and the colleges seem to be willing to do whatever it takes to cover their indiscretions when it comes to criminal activity and violating school and NCAA rules. What would've happened if part of the deal was, instead of suspending the cheer-team, we apologized to them for the set up in a subculture that never protected them and asked them for their little black book of customers so we could press charges? I'm sure you'd see a little bit more university cover-up then.

THE PROMISED ARMAGEDDON

In the fall of 2017, an article came out titled "**FBI Brings Armageddon to College Basketball, and it's Just the Tip of the Iceberg.**"[343] Basketball fans from far and wide waited for a massive bomb to explode as the FBI came strong with a press conference held by the interim U.S. Attorney General, Joon H. Kim.[344] The allegations were that several colleges were guilty of corruption, bribery, money-laundering, and fraud within the world of college basketball.[345] Adidas, the athletic shoe company was named as part of their criminal claims along with agents, programs, recruits and coaches.[346] Although schools weren't named, they were hinted at and the media had a field day playing "who done it" by the rumors and suspected allegations.[347]

For two years, the report states it had enough proof from wire taps, recorded conversations and financial transaction data to bring down the entire underbelly of college basketball.[348] As news speculated which school was which (six schools were originally listed in the FBI report) in the FBI's report, they assumed "University 6" was Coach Rick Pitino's squad—The University of Louisville.[349] The school was reported, in two separate instances, to pay high school recruits—eighteen year old boys—to attend the university and play basketball in the amounts of $100,000 and $150,000.[350] This comes as the second scandal with the Louisville University Men's Basketball program; the first in which they're still on probation started in 2010 and went through 2014.[351] During that time frame, Rick Pitino's assistant coach was caught paying strippers and prostitutes for high school recruits who came for their campus visit; some of the women that were sold in that exchange were underage, as were the basketball recruits.[352]

This scandal poses the most obvious question: why weren't trafficking charges filed against the University? And again, where'd the money come from?

According to the source reporting to ESPN with the knowledge of the investigation, Pitino didn't accept responsibility.[353] The anonymous source with knowledge of the situation was quoted saying, "This is not a guy who is turning his head to academic fraud; this is much worse than that. If any other coach was connected to this story, by now he'd have already been fired."[354] The money reported at that party raised eyebrows at the time; according to the source reporting to ESPN who had firsthand knowledge of the investigation the assistant coach, ". . .gave the players a stack of dollar bills ranging from $200 to $500. Everybody in the room got the money—the recruits and the current members of the team. Not only that, but McGee himself had his own stack of dollar bills. If this guy's spending $2,000 to $3,000 on a recruiting weekend, where's this money coming from?"[355] The woman who worked several parties also confirmed in her book, "Breaking Cardinal Rules: Basketball and the Escort Queen," that she'd been hired to work nearly two dozen parties at the college dorms for the basketball team and recruits and was hired by the basketball staff.[356] And although in the filing from the University, they claimed Coach Pitino had no knowledge of the sex parties, he couldn't get away with that for long; he was forced to resign with the new allegations and fresh investigation from the FBI.[357] The NCAA's original punishment for trafficking underage girls was a five-game suspension and four years' probation.[358] For corruption involving money however, he lost his job.[359]

This wasn't Pitino's first scandal; in 2009, he was accused of raping a woman in a hotel and getting her pregnant.[360] He claims the sex was consensual and she was blackmailing him for money, however, there was proof at some point that $3,000 was exchanged, and it was explained by Coach Pitino (who was also a father and husband at the time) that it was for the abortion—a pretty high price for an abortion when the woman would have only been one month pregnant.[361] As such, the FBI got involved with that case, and the woman was charged with extortion and lying to the FBI.[362] The report reads, "Sgt. Andy Abbott, the commander of the police department's sex offense unit, asked Cunagin Sypher during one interview why she waited until after she was indicted on the extortion charge to report her allegations. She gave varying answers, according to transcripts, saying she wanted to forget about it, then that Pitino threatened her and finally that 'they kept throwing crumbs to keep me happy.' She didn't say what they were, the newspaper reported."[363] The obvious question again then is, who's "they?"

With the amount of money a college men's Division 1 basketball (and/or football) program brings in to a school, it's no surprise that with this obvious cover-up, Pitino's program is said to be "one of the most successful in history on the court and for decades the most lucrative hoops program in America," according to a news report.[364] Other schools were listed in the intimidatingly titled article of the Armageddon of NCAA, including assistant coaches at Arizona, Auburn, Oklahoma State and USC who were all arrested.[365,366,367,368] Here's the irony: When shoe contracts, underhanded financial deals for players, bribes and dirty-handed financial gain are at play, people lose their jobs, get criminal charges, and their career is forever tarnished. However, when women and underage girls are being sold to college athletes, gang rape is the norm, and the players and the staff get a few game suspension (but the women get slut shamed)—the entire web of professionals are left with their reputations and careers protected and intact—we have a serious problem on our hands. Herein lies the system of trafficking.

The same subculture we've identified as sex slavery is the identical subculture operating in college sports: the breeding ground where rape is accepted and the universities allow it, donors pay for it, and universities create a system of covering up the crimes all for financial gain. Everyone involved is either in on the financial gain (which would make them traffickers) or threatened to underreport, don't report, look the other way, or cover up the rape cases all together. Whether "Police Officer Joe Shmow" and "Becky Smith" from the communications department who teaches a class where a student approaches her and reports the assault is blind or being paid off, they are still part of the system. If they don't blow the whistle, the system remains, and women and children are sold as slaves. It's the professionals who choose the loyalty of the system to protect their paycheck versus the truth and their obligation to fight for freedom that makes the difference. They're the lynchpin to pull in either the direction of safety for the women on their college campus with honest reporting wherein proper actions follow, or if the entire trafficking system is able to flourish. They have the power to choose safety and loyalty. That decision creates the following: athletes make the university an incredible amount of money in season tickets, the annual enrollment for the university increases due to their athletic success, the players and coaching staff get to ride above the law, adolescent athletes receive six-figure salaries which are illegally paid to their families, and they can have whatever woman they want—even if she says no. The top players know the university needs them because of the power they bring in making the establishment millions. If those in charge put the correct loyal staff in place, their system goes uninterrupted. If not, they're threatened—either the truth comes out and a revolution results, or the crooks behind the curtain keep their money in offshore accounts and bitcoins; all the while the victims of this horrendous crime are changed forever and not because they chose to be. Those involved hold the pin that keeps the wheel moving one way or the other. And the one with the most direct knowledge on any college campus is the Title IX Director.

PLAYING POLITICS

Much has changed on the political scene in the last decade with the switch of a President resulting in a new perspective on Title IX. President Obama and Vice President Joe Biden were vocal about the war on women's sexuality and civil rights on university and college campuses across the United States and communicated very clearly the weight and importance of Title IX enforcement to ensure the safety of women in educational atmospheres.[369] Under the United States Department of Education, in 2011 a very clear and concise twenty-page document called the "Dear Colleague Letter" was written.[370] The letter contains a very concise explanation of procedures on how to handle a hostile sexual environment.[371] It defines a clear policy and procedure on how to handle sexual discrimination and defines sexual violence as the term referring to the following:

> "physical sexual acts perpetrated against a person's will or where a person is incapable of giving consent due to the victim's use of drugs or alcohol. An individual also may be unable to give consent due to an intellectual or other disability. A number of different acts fall into the category of sexual violence, including rape, sexual assault, sexual battery, and sexual coercion. All such acts of sexual violence are forms of sexual harassment covered under Title IX. The statistics on sexual violence are both deeply troubling and a call to action for the nation."[372]

After a carefully spelled-out system to implement a safe learning environment after identifying that the rape culture had become an epidemic on the campuses of universities and colleges, the Office of Civil Rights added this in the document: "When conducting Title IX enforcement activities, OCR seeks to obtain voluntary compliance from recipients. When a recipient does not come into compliance voluntarily, OCR may initiate proceedings to withdraw Federal funding by the Department or refer the case to the U.S. Department of Justice for litigation."[373] This statement had colleges nervous—no money if you don't comply with the legal rights of women in a way that protects them from a hostile learning environment.

Once President Donald Trump took presidential office, he replaced many people in high positions, including the United States Secretary of Education.[374] In the early months of 2017, Betsy DeVos was sworn in off of a 51-50 vote.[375] With Vice President Mike Pence orchestrating the official tie breaker, the oath ceremony proceed making her the official Head of Education.[376] In September of 2017, the Office of the U.S. Department of Education came out with a mind-blowing move—they rescinded the *Dear Colleague Letter* from the Obama office expressing concerns and opinions that the document didn't give the man accused of sexual violence a fair shot at proving his innocence.[377] The *Dear Colleague Letter*, however, was very specific in its policies and procedures to ensure the accused was protected during the investigative process.[378] The Office of the U.S. Department of Education proceeded to release its own rendition of proper policy and procedure in a seven-page Q&A on Sexual Misconduct.[379] This new policy and procedure created a lot of grey area; decision-making is now up to the school regarding how much time it takes to investigate and report; it holds no responsibility to the college and university (the reason the Obama and the Department of Civil Rights created the *Dear Colleague Letter* to begin with), and it states that even if a perpetrator is accused over and over by different women, each accusation has to be considered individually.[380] Furthermore, there is nothing in the "improved" letter that calls any college or university into account for doing massive cover-ups—the one thing in Obama's letter (which caused hundreds of schools to suddenly comply with the original law to begin with) demanded.[381]

According to the seven-page Q&A, each university can proceed whenever they want and however they want, and even if they don't, there's no longer any financial consequence. In the wake of the Obama administration's solution to a problem we're all familiar with—college campuses are breeding grounds for sexual predators with massive amounts of money at stake that jeopardize and disregard the safety of our women—the Office of the U.S. Department of Education decides to put in practice the very thing that set women back, with no accountability for the true perpetrator—the system that holds it all together.[382] They relieve the lynchpin and make each Title IX Coordinator's responsibility easiest and irrelevant. The Office of the U.S. Department of Education gave the very system that blames women, allows rape, hires underage girls for sex, etc. the ability to do it without a system in place that holds them accountable—all in the name of the mighty dollar; true prostitution is ironically the one now leading the Education Department. The *Dear Colleague Letter* was said to have gone too far by not protecting the accused, however the woman who was placed as the head of the Civil-Rights Department, Candace Jackson, told *The Times* in an interview about women reporting sexual violence that "90 percent of campus accusations are over drunk breakup sex."[383,384]

In just a short few years, the Office of the U.S. Department of Education single-handedly dismantled the answer for unity and accountability of the system. Awareness and a very detailed action plan for educational institutions brought by Obama's Administration are completely dispelled by the hiring of someone who is blaming the very women taxpayers hire to protect. The reason Title IX needed to exist in the first place is because of the inequality and objectification of women; they weren't being protected and given equal treatment. In 1972 the law passed, and a woman takes office and desecrates on the efforts toward equality— the steps necessary to ensure the safety of women from soul murder— which was done in less than a year under a president who has a history of women accusing him of sexual violence and a pattern of public comments about his views, actions and treatment toward women that are congruent with the viewpoint of the objectification of women.[385]

DeVos stated that the reason a new policy is needed was to ensure each educational institution was "protecting both the accusers and the accused."[386] The *Dear Colleague Letter* already covered this in the recommended procedure by giving steps to ensure the truth was carefully extracted, and the victims that suffered at the hands of educational malpractice and cover-up schemes were finally getting the protection and attention due. The abused, according to the Office of the U.S. Department of Education's new rules, are now thrown into another loophole of trauma; she is just as suspect as the accused. The regulations are loose and the government once again fails to protect women who are in need of safety and equal treatment—their Civil Rights. Furthermore, the Office of the U.S. Department of Education also added a higher standard for proof that the woman was sexually assaulted in order for her to receive protection and safety.[387] It is now up to the school to decide, just like it is when they cover everything up.

The one factor both documents agree on is the responsibility of the school to investigate.[388,389] Now, when money is at stake from donors and ticket holders, they can cover up their sexual violence without fear that consequences from the government will transpire. It makes you wonder why the head of the U.S. Department of Education would do something— especially as a woman—that seems so obviously anti-female.

Just briefly, let us revisit the toxic ingredients to this madness? The head of the U.S. Department of Education is working directly with the

President's administration.[390] The President is notorious for sexually assaulting women and publicly bragging and justifying his actions.[391,392] Candice Jackson, who works under the head of the U.S. Department of Education as the head of the Civil Rights Department called the alleged victims of the President "fake victims."[393]

To justify the new Q&A, a fallacy was utilized saying that the amount of false reports on sex crimes is equivalent to the true reports.[394] The actual data is that only 2-8% of reports are false.[395,396] Why would the head of the U.S. Department of Education make such a smoke-and-mirrors effort? Could it be for the same reason the system is able to exist?

Knight In Shining Armor

DeVos is connected to a very powerfully structured organization that leads all the way to the top of our political system. Politics and sports are two of the social systems in which sex trafficking is enabled and encouraged to operate. By removing the responsibility of Title IX Coordinator (and like positions), the wheel stays intact, and no one knows anything other than what's reported. But the chips are falling, and individuals connected to both systems are becoming unveiled. In July of 2015, retired Indiana University basketball coach Bob Knight was invited to give a speech at the National Geospatial-Intelligence Agency (NGA), an arm of the Department of Defense that analyzes imagery of the Earth's surface in order to serve national operations of intelligence.[397] According to documents obtained by the Washington Post and interviews with members of the agency, Knight was accused of **groping at least four women** while he was at the NGA.[398]

According to the Post, Knight **first made inappropriate remarks about and touched a female employee** who had been sent to pick him up from the airport.[399] In an interview with *The Washington Post*, the woman said that Knight commented on her legs and then touched her shoulder in a way "you don't do to a female."[400]

After arriving at the NGA, Knight was greeted by **another female employee whom he allegedly gripped by the side of the chest and lifted off the ground.**[401] Later in the day, just before going on stage to give his speech, Knight allegedly groped another female NGA employee's derrière *The Washington Post*:

> "Moments before he walked into the auditorium, Knight suddenly put his arm around her shoulders and groped her on the buttocks," the woman told *The Washington Post* in an interview. She said she was "so startled that she could barely maintain her composure."[402]

> "You can shake my hand. You can give me a hug. But you don't get to feel me up on my body," she said.[403]

A male NGA employee, Marc Byers, reported to a supervisor that he witnessed the incident.[404] In **a signed statement** provided to investigators as part of the discrimination complaint, he said **he was standing directly behind the woman when he saw Knight grab her on the buttocks multiple times.**[405]

The final incident allegedly occurred while Knight was signing autographs after his speech. At this time, **a fourth woman claims that Knight smacked her on the butt** as she reached the front of the autograph line.[406]

According to the documents obtained by *The Washington Post*, an investigation into Knight's conduct was opened by the Army's Criminal Investigation Command but was later handed off to the FBI, because Knight is not a government employee.[407] **The FBI did nothing with the case until April 2016,** at which point agents flew to Montana to interview Knight.[408] **The former coach denied any wrongdoing during his interview, and the investigation was closed shortly after that."**[409]

In one story, we see the history of politics and athletics working hand in hand. It must be questioned to begin with, why was a former basketball coach speaking at a spy conference to begin with?

(Text Bolded by Author)

BIRDS OF A FEATHER....

Coach Knight endorsed President Trump when he began to run for the presidency and spoke at his rallies across the country, saying he was the "most prepared man in history to be the President of the United States."[410] As someone who only looks at X's and O's (as basketball coaches do) and has been out of the limelight for years living a retired life in a home in Montana, what qualifies his statement as fact in regards to political preparation? Furthermore, let it be noted, Bob Knight is infamous for his statement to Connie Chung in an interview where he said, "I think that if rape is inevitable, relax and enjoy it."[411]

Bob Knight was a Big Ten Basketball Coach for Indiana University just like Tom Izzo from MSU.[412] Tom Izzo's boss, former President Lou Anne Simon, recently resigned from the school's presidential office over the cover-up at MSU's athletic department. Just two days before the new Title IX Q&A was released, DeVos met with (former) President Lou Anne Simon - the title of the article reads:

> "**Betsy DeVos Rolled Back Title IX Protections Two Days After Hanging Out With MSU President**"[413]

Interestingly enough, another article came out with this headline:

> "**U.S. Education Secretary Betsy DeVos says agency investigating Michigan State**."[414]

If the Baylor University rape scandal is any indicator to the MSU scandal currently unfolding, it's important to remember Baylor's pattern. As they continued to cover up the scandal by using fresh faces in the hiring and firing of different positions within the athletic department, the root was exposed when the system's scapegoats spoke out. The breaking of loyalty from their 'higher-ups' broke their silence, and pointed to the object worth $332 Million that contained all the answers; the Pepper Hamilton Investigation Reports found its way into the Supreme Court.

Another related article headlined stating: **"In Larry Nassar probe, Michigan Attorney General Schuette eyes former MSU staffers"**[415] When this article ran, and other news broke out about Nassar's sentencing, the interim President at MSU said Schuette pulled a "cheap political stunt for the media."[417] Another headline article reads: **"Investigators execute search warrant at MSU,"** and according to the Lansing Journal, "The Department of Attorney General Special Agents and Michigan State Police removed records and what appeared to be a flash drive from the Hannah Administration Building and Fee Hall, the Lansing State Journal reported Friday."[418] According to the pattern, why did the Attorney General's Office rush in for documents? Could the information on that flash drive be the equivalent to the hidden information in the Pepper-Hamilton Investigation Reports? Are these the questions we should ask before we have something bigger than a Baylor scandal on our hands? Is this another cover-up in the making?

Mr., Mr., Where's My Sister?

5. Mr., Mr., Where's My Sister?

"Because the problem with prostitution always comes from one thing without which it could not exist at all: the men. A man who pays for sex knows that the woman he's paying anticipates no satisfaction from the encounter beyond a financial reward that she may direly need (after all, there's no need to pay if she was having sex for her own genuine pleasure), and yet he doesn't find anything obnoxious about purchasing her consent. Maybe it's even a turn-on for him. How much do you have to dehumanise a woman to think it acceptable to use her like that? How much easier to be violent to someone you already see as inferior." -Sarah Ditum [419]

Cinnamon

Let's say you're with your buddies that you haven't seen in some time. It's guys night out. The wives, girlfriends, and kiddos are home tucked away asleep—meaning you have the night off from familial and professional pressure. Five of you are having an amazing time over cocktails, and just as the bill is paid, the synergy of reminiscing from college or high school hasn't died down, and the boys want to keep you out for "just one more round." Harmless fun it seems as everyone jumps into a taxi and goes to another spot for last call. When they pull up, it's the local strip club. Knowing you're not a frequent, but, again, you remind yourself that it is just harmless fun; you exit the cab with the guys and head in for a night you'll end up telling your wife about because Jim will probably do something for the books. He's always been the one to stir up trouble and when he's there, the life of the party ends up going down in history for something even your wife will find amusing. As the cover charge is paid, you've already decided you're only going to stay for no more than an hour before heading back home to your beautiful wife and kids. As you walk in and the waitress takes your order, you look around, and the bar is packed. Why wouldn't it be? It's a Friday night and this is "just what men do." Suddenly, the DJ makes the announcement, "Gentleman put your hands together and get your dollar bills ready. . . here comes. . .Cinnamon!!!" The crowd erupts: As you silently judge the piggish men while reminding yourself how grateful your wife should be that at least you're not like "those sleazy men." Your mind shifts and you remember how you need to remember to call your mother and have your wife thank her for raising such a gentleman. With a smile looming, you look up to see the star of the show Cinnamon, and in a split second you come to grips with the fact that you don't need to wait to call your mother in the morning, because she's the one on stage. Cinnamon is your mother.

I can imagine the sheer horror and rejection of the thought that your mother would ever do anything like that. Maybe you're not moved; the relationship between you and your mother is strained or you never knew her. So to those of you with no attachment to your mom, let's make it fair. Maybe it's your sister. Your daughter. Your wife. Anyone of those on the list would never cause you to feel an OUNCE of how you felt when Cinnamon was just a girl naked on stage and you are with your boys for "harmless fun." But please consider the fact that Cinnamon IS someone's mom, sister, daughter, wife etc. The emotional difference in your response to your own connection versus just a beautiful woman that loves her job is the difference between the problem and the solution.

Social Pressure and Cultural Power

The statistics on men purchasing sex are telling. Taking a look at the majority of reports from online stories of trafficking busts, the consumer is consistently reported as a stereotypical white, educated, married man.[420] The one portrayed as the ideal male in mainstream is the exact same one paying for the system to exist. The American white, educated, married man is the rapist fueling the existence of slavery.

If we're to try and understand the causality of why men purchase sex, the debate would be never-ending. People's thought would take too long and be too subjective when discussing the matter at hand. It is important to note, though, that if we step back and realize that if the "supply" exists (the woman) and the "system" exists (rape culture) but if the "demand" doesn't exist, the entire problem is solved. The question we need to ask ourselves then is, *How do we as a society change the culture to free men so women are free?*

According to one study, the percentage of men who buy sex per country varies. The article reports:

> "Mansson reported that 14 percent of Dutch men have bought sex as compared with nearly 40 percent of men in Spain. (Prostitution is legal in both countries.) And according to HYDRA, a Berlin-based organization that provides legal advice and other aid to prostitutes, up to three quarters of men in Germany, which also has legalized prostitution, have paid for sexual services. Meanwhile other estimates for Germany put the proportion far lower, at about one fifth. In Thailand, where prostitution is illegal but socially accepted, one study suggested that a whopping 95 percent of men have slept with a prostitute."[421]

Based on these stats, we can immediately point out the obvious; the lie that "men will be men" cannot explain why in certain countries the percentage of their male population who purchase sex is low and in others high.

Another article reinstates the previous point: "'The biggest thing curtailing their behavior is to have it publicized so people in their workplace and the community know what they're doing,' Peters said."[422]

Just as they socially accept sex for sale in Thailand, 95% of men partake of the purchase even though it's illegal.[423] When purchasers are publicly shamed by their decision, the rate of being a "frequent shopper" drops dramatically.[424,425]

This identifies where the solution to the entire system lies; in the hands of our society as a whole. By setting a cultural expectation that no longer blames the victim and no longer tolerates men seeing women as an object but a person, we would pull the plug on this insidious crime. It is literally up to all of us to solve the problem. When we demand that both men and women stop competing, we simultaneously expect that men protect women as sisters, mothers, daughters, who are equally valuable and not for sale, sex slavery becomes obsolete. Instead of a hierarchy, we live in interdependence with respect to one another because everyone is created uniquely. On the other hand, If we don't work toward that and stay in silence, we are part of the problem. More on this when we conclude.

GREED

6. Greed

"Growth for the sake of growth is the ideology of the cancer cell."-Edward Abbey [426]

When the financial numbers are shown, the motive becomes obvious; it clarifies the obvious reason behind the crime. Currently, the numbers are misleading and show a massive gap in the unrealistic data. We can conclude this by looking at the cases we've explained in this document already and the money spent which is a more accurate reflection on the economy of the rape culture.

The Reported Numbers

"In 2014, the Urban Institute studied the underground commercial sex economy in eight U.S. cities and estimated that this illicit activity generated between $39.9 million and $290 million in revenue depending on the city. According to the study, pimps in one city earned an average of $32,833 per week. It is within this economy that sex trafficking thrives, and with this potential for earnings, sex trafficking is considered a low-risk, high-reward endeavor."[427]

The Real Numbers

Sex Trafficking is an economic pillar of the country. If one lower socio-economic trafficking ring in the country has 10 girls, and each girl makes $200 each time she meets with a client, and assuming she keeps a schedule for her trafficker of 10 tricks per day (remember some appointments only last 15 minutes), we'd do simple math and see the figures are staggering. Please also keep in mind, this is on the low end of the rape culture. Just like in the mainstream culture there are different socio-economic ranges, as it is in the subculture (i.e. blue collar vs. white collar etc.). Take $2,000 (again a low number) and multiply that by 365 days in a year. That would make $730,000 in a year for one girl. Multiply that number by 10 girls which would be $7,300,000 for one trafficking ring of ten girls. If we take that number and assume that for every state (which again puts us as an unrealistically low number) in this country there are ten trafficking rings of the same size (again a low number). We then multiply $7,300,000 by four and then, per each state (50), we come up with a staggering amount of financial movement. The numbers are as follows:

$200 x 10 clients/day x 365 days=$730,000 per year

$730,000 x 10 girls= $7,300,000 per year for 1 ring.

$7,300,000 x4 cities x50 states = $1,460,000,000 per year.

These are domestic numbers in the "Land of the Free"—the rape culture's economy spelled out in the United States from the lower socioeconomic trafficking rings.

There were actually 10 rings I was made aware of in the 3 weeks I assisted law enforcement. The city had a population of just over 75,000 people; a small town where this economy is producing well over what middle and upper-class America understands—at least those that aren't participating.

The people making the most money from sex trafficking do not want the real statistics to be reported because they are the ones at the top of the totem pole orchestrating the entire hierarchy of sex slavery. They're the top dog in terms of power and socioeconomic status making money off the lower socio-economic population. If you research the money being made, the statistics being reported, and the victims of those being bought and sold in sex slavery, you'll find the reports are congruent with the lower-class population. This is designed to cause the diversion that furthers their financial agenda. This is why, when the word "pimp" is used, the general assumption assumes we're discussing an African American male in a fur coat, alligator shoes and a pimp cane. This is the stereotype being pushed, so we never really see who's making the gain from selling people.

Keep on Sailin' Sailor

To further the evidence that anchors the previous section, the numbers speak again. In the Rick Pitino scandal of 2014 where coaches were hiring sex workers to entertain their players and recruits by hiring some underage and above age women to strip and provide sex for the men, the report concerned the public (the question was posed in one of the articles) and had them asking the same question: *Where did this money come from?*[428]

As stated in chapter four, the money reported at that party raised eyebrows at the time. According to the source reporting to ESPN who had firsthand knowledge of the investigation, the assistant coach, ". . .gave the players a stack of dollar bills ranging from $200 to $500. Everybody in the room got the money—the recruits and the current members of the team. Not only that, but McGee himself had his own stack of dollar bills. If this guy's spending $2,000 to $3,000 on a recruiting weekend, where's this money coming from?"[429]

Per the NCAA rules, there are 34 weekends per year recruits can be contacted. [430,431] If each weekend, the team holds 1 party with 5 women hired, and according to the report this happened between 2010 and 2014 (please remember some of the recruits and the women hired were underage),[432] this is how the math goes:

Louisville team has an average of 15 players per year.[433] We will assume they follow NCAA rules and only 12 recruits are able to do official visits per year.[434] To ensure our reporting numbers are congruent with the last mathematical equation, we will assume each party has 1 recruit and the team along with 1 coach for a total of 17 men.

17 men x $350/each player (median of the $200-$500 reported)=$5,950/party (i.e. recruiting visit)

12 recruiting visits / year x$5,950= $71,400 annually

If we replace the $350 average, assume they're following NCAA recruiting regulations of only 12 official recruiting visits/year, and assume only 1 coach is orchestrating and organizing these parties, however because we've assumed the obvious contradiction that they're following rules, let's overcompensate and put the figure per player at $500. That puts us over $100,000.

If we can assume that there are at least 10 schools in the country hosting these parties based on the evidence of other criminal activity going on, we have hit over $1 million dollars on an unrealistically low math equation.

17 men x$500= $8500

12 recruiting visits/year=$102,000

102,000 x 10 schools in the country= $1.2 million.

Stuart Dunnings III: Math equations

Let's not forget about the Prosecuting Attorney, Stuart Dunnings III who had numbers also reported in the affidavit.[435] Here's how those numbers break down: W-1 reported she'd have appointments with Dunnings 3-4 times per week and she reported he spent $200 for each time. Here's how that math plays out:

$200/hour x 3 days = $600/week. $600 x 52 weeks/: **$31,200. per year**

She also reported he'd paid her rent, which increases the number, along with the price of the hotel spent, gas money, and extra things he'd paid for during their visits (lunch, etc.)[436] We will say the average motel is $50/check in.[437] We won't include gas, and we will assume lunch cost $20 and also only calculate that ⅓ times they met for the sale of sex, they ate together.

$150/week in hotel x 52 wks= **$7,800**

$20/week in food x52 wks= **$1,040**

Rent/month (assuming the lowest end of any rent possible) $100/26 weeks (even more wiggle room for argument to low ball the number assuming he only helped her half of the year) **$2,600**

Grand total on W-1=$42,640 /year.[438]

Please also keep in mind, these reports were from Dunnings trafficking and paying for sex over multiple years.[439]

W-2: stated in the affidavit that her prices were, "$100 per half hour, $160 per hour, and $140 per hour for multiple hours; Dunnings typically gave her $200 per occasion. Had commercial sex over 200 times"[440]

If Dunnings gave her $200/appointment, they had over 200 appointments

= $40,000 (at least)

She also reported he spent $80/week for methadone treatments which is used to detox off heroin.[441] The professional medical reports state that it is mandatory for the first 90 days with at least a year of treatment in order for it to work.[442]

For methadone treatment, Dunnings spent $80/week x 52 weeks=

$4,160/year

W-2 also reported he'd paid her cell phone bill, took her grocery shopping and paid for her to have a YMCA membership.[443] Here are those numbers assuming very low averages:

Cell phone bill: $50 per month x 12= **$600 per year**

Grocery Shopping: $100 per month = **$1,200 per year**

YMCA: $52 x12= **$624 per year**

Grand total on W-2: $46,632 per year

W-3: She reported she'd only met with Dunnings 5 times and he spent $200 each time.[444]

Total for W-3: $1,000

W-4: W-4 reported that Dunnings was a regular customer (someone who is consistent client over a given time).[445] She didn't list the amount he spent, however per his pattern, we can assume his $200 amount was used again. Because it's hard to assume her reference to his sex for hire practice making him a "regular," we will once again assume on the lower end of the figures and say 2x/wk.

$200 x 2 times/week= 400/wk x52= $20,800/year

Total for W-4: $20,800/year

W-5: W-5 only reported meeting with Dunnings where he paid her $150 for the 15 minute meetings they'd arranged and they only met for sex 1 time.[446]

Total for W-5: $150

W-6: W-6's case was a little sticky when totaling up the numbers due to the fact that he was using intimidation on someone because of her financial position and because of her situation with her child's father.[447] She was in a vulnerable position, and since he was the Prosecutor, she knew if she refused to give him what he wanted, he had the power to use it against her and have her kid taken away.[448] She reported he gave her $600 every 2 weeks, listed 2 lunches at a cafe', gifts, and some of her bills.[449] The hotels Dunnings took her to for commercial sex acts were the Fairfield Inn (average $100/night) and Causeway Bay Hotel ($110/night) (although it was also stated sometimes at a trailer in Holt, MI; the same place Larry Nassar lived).[450,451,452] Here's how the math plays out:

$300/wk x 52wks= $15,600

$20/ 2x lunch= $40

gifts= can't assume based on lack of info. (i.e. term too broad)

Fairfield Inn 6/year x $100= $600

Causeway Bay Hotel 6x/yr x $110= $660

Bills= $50/month x12= $600

Total for W-6 = $17,500/ year

Note: Dunnings was reported purchasing sex from the first 5 women from 2010 through 2015.[453] For W-6, that only lasted for 2 years.[454] Let's do a grand total by adding the numbers reported times the years it occurred.

W-1: $167,440 x5= $213,200

W-2: $46,632 x5= $233,160

W-3: $1,000 x5 = $5,000

W-4: $20,800 x5 = $104,000

W-5: $150 (only reported one exchange) $150

W-6: $17,500 x2= $35,000

TOTAL=**$590,510.**

The total is staggering, especially considering the annual salary reported in 2016 that Mr. Dunnings was receiving was $132,000 and was reported to be the highest paid employee in Ingham County.[455,456] Can someone please explain to me where this man was able to provide for his family and spend over a half million dollars on sex when the total salary over the five year span only equated to $660,000?[457] We're once again left with the question; where'd the money come from?

THE REAL LOCKER ROOM

Don't forget the "True Story" we mentioned about The MSU football team either, when they came into the strip club off a private bus and all players spent hundreds each in 90 minutes. Please keep in mind this is happening on that end too and there are a considerably larger amount of football players than basketball players each year on each team.

The rape culture overlaps within sports, politics, education, and religion and all other systems within our society. As we see, it's being consistently swept under the rug. If the male players and athletes are the clients, and per the research we've identified that social acceptability is the deciding factor on whether men will purchase sex, it is literally up to the culture to create a counterculture in each system and realm to alleviate the idea that it is acceptable to rape women and children. The question then, is how.

Fixing the Problem: Now What? What Now?

Last-second Shot

7. LAST-SECOND SHOT

There is a scientific experiment called the Perceptual Adaptation Experiment that summarizes the problem we've discussed and locates the solution needed to abolish slavery.[458] An American Psychologist named George Stratton used himself as a test subject and trained one of his eyes to see things upside-down.[459] In order to do this, he placed a black cloth over one eye and a lens over his other eye which inverted his vision.[460] By the fourth day, things we're still upside-down, however on the fifth day, things were upright, except when he focused on them, in which they'd go upside down again.[461] After only five days, his perception had already flipped everything upside down.[462]

Because each culture is based off the agreed collective perception, and with the totality of the information provided in previous chapters, we can safely conclude that what's needed is a change in perspective. In other words, the subculture is able to exist from an upside-down view of the male/female dynamic. How then do we flip the perspective from greed to love/objectivity to individuality/slavery to freedom? What then is the mechanism needed to flip it all right-side up again?

FOR THE WIN

We must locate this obscured mechanism by tracing it back to where it started. Since the sex for sale subculture was created by the mainstream culture, it's located at the root of our own cultural paradigm. By the mainstream social agreement we weren't considering (prior to the information provided in the previous chapters), we now understand that we've had the power to change it all along. The one to change the outcome has the power to direct the trajectory of the future. The subculture, being an intensified expression of the mainstream culture is really a mirror or aspect of our everyday unconscious agreement. It is sped up inside of time as an example of what we've created and what we've systematically accepted. It's time to wake up and decided to consciously divorce our passive non-resistant paradigm and create a counterculture of true freedom.

The working parts of the entire subculture can be boiled down to three main components: the system, the supply, and the demand. There is one ingredient that, if subtracted from the whole, makes the subculture obsolete. If we subtract the demand, there is no more need for supply, and the entire system collapses. The answer is in the demand. But it goes a bit further. In chapter 5, we explained that the power to move this particular component one way or the other is contained in the overall social acceptability. If the mainstream culture says it's ok, regardless of legal ramifications, the entire subculture is created and thriving. If there is a demand for it, the system is big business resulting in the anarchy of a woman's original design; it must be tampered with and destroyed in order to supply what the man is demanding from her.

If the demand is determined by the common approval, then the demand becomes obsolete by a common cultural disapproval. The main component that the subculture hangs on is the cultural shift of agreement in a man's role and how he views the value and worth of women. The answer is simple, and we have the power to steer the ship on which direction we want this to go. If we want to turn the entire thing right-side up again, it's imperative that men shift their overall perspective on the male/female dynamic. As that happens, women in mainstream also need to shed the lens that lies about who they are individually and as a whole. When you know you're worth something more, you don't accept something less. By creating a new standard on how we perceive each other, evolutionary jumps happen and change the course of our families, communities, countries and the world. It's time to make the shift.

. . . . GAME OVER . . . .

WORKS CITED

1. Cecchet, S. J., & Thoburn, J. (2014). The psychological experience of child and adolescent sex trafficking in the United States: Trauma and resilience in survivors. *Psychological Trauma: Theory, Research, Practice, and Policy, 6*(5), 482-493. http://dx.doi.org/10.1037/a0035763

2. "Albert Einstein Quotes." *BrainyQuote*, Xplore, www.brainyquote.com/quotes/albert_einstein_385842.

3. Johnson, Kimberly B. "Laws In 35 U.S. States Let Cops Have Sex With Someone In Their Custody." *Konbini United States*, 9 Feb. 2018, www.konbini.com/us/lifestyle/35-states-let-cops-sex-someone-custody/.

4. "Subculture." *Wikipedia*, Wikimedia Foundation, 13 Feb. 2018, en.wikipedia.org/wiki/Subculture.

5. Bicchieri, Cristina, and Ryan Muldoon. "Social Norms." *Stanford Encyclopedia of Philosophy*, Stanford University, 1 Mar. 2011, plato.stanford.edu/entries/social-norms/.

6. "Subculture." *Wikipedia*, Wikimedia Foundation, 13 Feb. 2018, en.wikipedia.org/wiki/Subculture.

7. "Survival of the Fittest." *Wikipedia*, Wikimedia Foundation, 12 Feb. 2018, en.wikipedia.org/wiki/Survival_of_the_fittest.

11. O'Brien, Cathy, and Mark Phillips. *Trance Formation of America:* Reality Marketing, 2001.

12. "Understanding the Teen Brain ." *Understanding the Teen Brain - Health Encyclopedia - University of Rochester Medical Center,* www.urmc.rochester.edu/encyclopedia/content.aspx?ContentTypeI D=1&ContentID=3051

13. Rohin, Wendy, et al. "Brain Development of Children from 0-6 Years - Facts Every Parent Should Know." *ADAM & Mila*, 29 Aug. 2017, www.adam-mila.com/brain-development-children-0-6-years/.

14. Lisa McCann, I & Pearlman, Laurie. (1992). Constructivist Self-Development Theory: A Theoretical Framework for Assessing and Treating Traumatized College Students. *Journal of American college health : J of ACH.* 40. 189-96.

15. Epstein, S., & Erskine, N. (1983). The development of personal theories of reality. In D. Magnusson & V. Allen (Eds.), *Human development: An interactional perspective* (pp. 133-147). New York: Academic Press

16. J. Mahoney, Michael. (1981). Clinical Psychology and Scientific Inquiry. *International Journal of Psychology - INT J PSYCHOL.* 16. 257-274.

17,18. Piaget, J. "Intellectual Evolution from Adolescence to Adulthood." *Human Development*, vol. 15, no. 1, 1972, pp. 1–12., doi:10.1159/000271225.

19. "Jean Piaget." *Jean Piaget | Cognitive Theory | Simply Psychology*, www.simplypsychology.org/piaget.html.

20. "Chapter 3: Section 1: Introduction to Development, Personality, and Stage Theories." *AllPsych*, allpsych.com/psychology101/personality/.

21. "95 Percent of Brain Activity Is beyond Our Conscious Awareness." *Neurosciences UX*, 9 Aug. 2008, www.simplifyinginterfaces.com/2008/08/01/95-percent-of-brain-activity-is-beyond-our-conscious-awareness/.

22. "Repetition Compulsion." *Wikipedia*, Wikimedia Foundation, 13 Feb. 2018, en.wikipedia.org/wiki/Repetition_compulsion.

23. "FBI Busts Sex Trafficking Ring Selling 3-Month-Old, 5-Year-Old Sister for $600." *Fox News*, FOX News Network,

24. "3 Ohio Pastors Indicted on Child Sex Trafficking Conspiracy." *fox8.Com*, 15 Nov. 2017, fox8.com/2017/11/15/3-ohio-pastors-indicted-on-child-sex-trafficking-conspiracy/.

25. "Cop Whose Job Was to Bust Prostitutes, Exposed as a Pimp in Massive Sex Trafficking Ring." *The Daily Liberator*, 4 Feb. 2016, www.thedailyliberator.com/cop-whose-job-bust-prostitutes-exposed-pimp-massive-sex-trafficking-ring/.

26. Pitts, Fadell. "Youth Leader, Coach, EMT among Nearly a Dozen Arrested in Kingsport Human Trafficking Case." *WJHL*, 15 Aug. 2017, wjhl.com/2017/08/15/tbi-kingsport-police-investigate-human-trafficking-details-revealed-at-news-conference-today/.

27. Ktrk. "Katy Volleyball Coach Arrested in Sex Trafficking Sting." *ABC13 Houston*, 12 Feb. 2017, abc13.com/news/katy-volleyball-coach-arrested-in-sex-trafficking-sting/1747046/.

28. Sorci, Anthony. "High School Coach Arrested for Pimping after Panicked 17-Year-Old Calls 911." *Sacbee*, The Sacramento Bee, www.sacbee.com/news/local/crime/article192166194.html.

29. Shrier, Adam. "Massive Human Trafficking Sting in Texas Leads to 61 Arrests." *NY Daily News*, NEW YORK DAILY NEWS, 28 June 2016, www.nydailynews.com/news/crime/massive-human-trafficking-sting-texas-leads-61-arrests-article-1.2691718

30. "US Parents Sold Daughters to Child Pornographer." *Stuff*, www.stuff.co.nz/world/americas/80857166/us-parents-sold-daughters-to-child-pornographer.

31. Nguyen, Jeannie. "Albuquerque Doctor Arrested on Child Prostitution Charges." *KRQE News 13*, 10 Feb. 2017, krqe.com/2017/02/10/albuquerque-doctor-arrested-on-child-prostitution-charges/.

32. Gross, Bob. "Port Huron Doctor Faces Prostitution Charges." *Detroit Free Press*, Detroit Free Press, 15 Nov. 2016, www.freep.com/story/news/local/michigan/2016/11/15/port-huron-doctor-faces-prostitution-charges/93908382/.

33-51. Dixon, Sandra. "How Pedophiles Groom Our Children And Us!" *Preda Foundation, Inc.*, www.preda.org/world/how-pedophiles-groom-our-children-and-us/.

52. "What Is Human Trafficking?" *Department of Homeland Security*, 21
Nov. 2016, www.dhs.gov/blue-campaign/what-human-trafficking.

53. Freeman, Mike. "Getting a Grip on Recruiting Parties." *The New York
Times*, The New York Times, 20 Nov. 2002,
www.nytimes.com/2002/11/21/sports/getting-a-grip-on-recruiting-
parties.html.

54,55. "Title IX - Gender Equity in Education." *American Civi
l Liberties Union*, www.aclu.org/title-ix-gender-equity-education.

56. "Title IX." *Know Your IX*, www.knowyourix.org/college-
resources/title-ix/.

57. United States. Dept. of Education. Office of Civil Rights. *Questions
and Answers on Title IX and Sexual Violence*. 2017. Web.
September 2017.

58. "Federal Laws." *StopBullying.gov*,
www.stopbullying.gov/laws/federal/index.html.

59,60. "Title IX Signed Statement." *KNOw MORE*,
knowmore.fsu.edu/title-ix/title-ix-signed-statement/.

61. United States. Dept. of Education. Office of Civil Rights. *Q&A on
Campus Sexual Misconduct* By Assistant Secretary. 2014. Web. 29
April 2014.

62. Delmore, Erin. "Will Betsy DeVos's Title IX Decision Really Make Schools Less Safe For Women?" *Bustle*, Bustle, 22 Dec. 2017, www.bustle.com/p/will-betsy-devoss-title-ix-decision-really-make-schools-less-safe-for-women-2435402.

63. Dixon, Sandra. "How Pedophiles Groom Our Children And Us!" *Preda Foundation, Inc.*, www.preda.org/world/how-pedophiles-groom-our-children-and-us/.

64. *Title Ix Investigator Salary*, www.payscale.com/research/US/Job=Title_Ix_Investigator/Salary.

65-67. Sokolow, B., Lewis, W., Schuster, S., Swinton, D. & Van Brunt, B. (2015). ATIXA Member Survey. www.atixa.org https://atixa.org/wordpress/wp-content/uploads/2012/01/Survey-Summary-B.pdf

68. Mencarini, Matt. "Schuette: Nassar Is 'a Monster' and More Charges Coming." *Lansing State Journal*, Lansing, 22 Feb. 2017, www.lansingstatejournal.com/story/news/local/2017/02/22/former-msu-doctor-larry-nassar-faces-23-new-sexual-assault-charges/98220438/.

69. Reid, Scott. "Plea Bargain for Ex-USA Gymnastics Team Doctor Accused of Sexually Abusing Gymnasts a 'Stunning Betrayal'." *Orange County Register*, Orange County Register, 10 July 2017, www.ocregister.com/2017/07/09/attorney-for-alleged-sexual-abuse-victims-labels-larry-nassars-plea-bargain-a-stunning-betrayal/.

70. "Out of Balance: An IndyStar Investigation into USA Gymnastics."
Out of Balance: An IndyStar Investigation into USA Gymnastic,
interactives.indystar.com/news/standing/OutOfBalanceSeries/inde
x2.html.

71. "Who Is Larry Nassar? Timeline of His Career, Prison Sentences."
USA Today, Gannett Satellite Information Network,
www.usatoday.com/pages/interactives/larry-nassar-timeline/.

72-96. "Out of Balance: An IndyStar Investigation into USA Gymnastics."
Out of Balance: An IndyStar Investigation into USA Gymnastic,
interactives.indystar.com/news/standing/OutOfBalanceSeries/inde
x2.html.

97. Haxel, Christopher, and Matt Mencarini. "MSU Fires Doctor Facing
Sexual Assault Allegations." *Lansing State Journal*, Lansing, 20
Sept. 2016,
www.lansingstatejournal.com/story/news/local/2016/09/20/msu-
fires-doctor-facing-sexual-assault-allegations/90734818/.

98. Mencarini, Matt. "At MSU: Assault, Harassment and Secrecy."
Lansing State Journal, Lansing, 25 Jan. 2018,
www.lansingstatejournal.com/story/news/local/2016/12/15/michig
an-state-sexual-assault-harassment-larry-nassar/94993582/.

99-114. "Human Trafficking Investigation Results In Criminal Charges
Against Ingham County Prosecutor Stuart Dunnings." *SOM -
Human Trafficking Investigation Results In Criminal Charges
Against Ingham County Prosecutor Stuart Dunnings*,
www.michigan.gov/som/0,4669,7-192-47796-378930--,00.html.

115,116. 54A Judicial District 30 Judicial Circuit. *People of the State of Michigan v Stuart Dunnings, III and Steven Dunnings*. Mar. 2016, www.michigan.gov/documents/ag/Stuart_Dunnings-Affidavit_-_54A_-_Dunnings_516941_7.pdf.

117. Hinkley, Justin A., and Matt Mencarini. "Stuart Dunnings' 20 Years of Work Mired in Controversy." *Lansing State Journal*, Lansing, 24 May 2016, www.lansingstatejournal.com/story/news/local/watchdog/2016/05/19/before-prostitution-charges-20-years-ups-and-downs-dunnings/83385198/.

118,119. "Disgraced Ingham County Prosecutor Takes Plea Deal In Prostitution Case." CBS Detroit, 2 Aug. 2016, detroit.cbslocal.com/2016/08/02/disgraced-ingham-county-prosecutor-takes-plea-deal-in-prostitution-case/.

120-125. 54A Judicial District 30 Judicial Circuit. *People of the State of Michigan v Stuart Dunnings, III and Steven Dunnings*. Mar. 2016, www.michigan.gov/documents/ag/Stuart_Dunnings-Affidavit_-_54A_-_Dunnings_516941_7.pdf.

126. Staff, 6 News Web. "UPDATE: Former Prosecutor Stuart Dunnings III Sentenced to 3 Years Probation, 1 Year Jail." *WLNS*, 22 Nov. 2016, wlns.com/2016/11/22/former-prosecutor-stuart-dunnings-iii-sentenced-to-3-years-probation-1-year-jail/.

127. 54A Judicial District 30 Judicial Circuit. *People of the State of Michigan v Stuart Dunnings, III and Steven Dunnings*. Mar. 2016, www.michigan.gov/documents/ag/Stuart_Dunnings-Affidavit_-_54A_-_Dunnings_516941_7.pdf.

128. Staff, 6 News Web. "UPDATE: Former Prosecutor Stuart Dunnings III Sentenced to 3 Years Probation, 1 Year Jail." *WLNS*, 22 Nov. 2016, wlns.com/2016/11/22/former-prosecutor-stuart-dunnings-iii-sentenced-to-3-years-probation-1-year-jail/.

129. Staff, 6 News Web. "UPDATE: Former Prosecutor Stuart Dunnings III Sentenced to 3 Years Probation, 1 Year Jail." *WLNS*, 22 Nov. 2016, wlns.com/2016/11/22/former-prosecutor-stuart-dunnings-iii-sentenced-to-3-years-probation-1-year-jail/.

130. "MSU Doctor's Alleged Victims Talked for 20 Years. Was Anyone Listening?" *MLive.com*, 2 Jan. 2018, www.mlive.com/news/index.ssf/page/msu_doctor_alleged_sexual_assault.html.

131,132,133. Mencarini, Matt. "Attorney: MSU Failed to 'Adequately Investigate' 2014 Nassar Complaint." *Lansing State Journal*, Lansing, 20 Mar. 2017, www.lansingstatejournal.com/story/news/local/2017/03/20/attorney-msu-failed-adequately-investigate-2014-nassar-complaint/99413154/.

134. Connor, Tracy. "Gymnastics Scandal: Dr. Larry Nassar's Fellow Doctor Rebuked by MSU." *NBCNews.com*, NBCUniversal News Group, 21 Mar. 2017, www.nbcnews.com/news/us-news/gymnastics-scandal-dr-larry-nassar-s-fellow-doctor-rebuked-msu-n736151.

135. Mencarini, Matt. "MSU Doctor Resigned after Removing Nassar Patient Files." *Lansing State Journal*, Lansing, 18 Mar. 2017, www.lansingstatejournal.com/story/news/local/2017/03/17/msu-doctor-resigned-after-removing-nassar-patient-files/99316854/.

136. Meyers, Dvora. "Michigan State Can't Bury Its Role In The Largest Sex Abuse Scandal In Sports History." *Deadspin*, Deadspin.com, 14 Dec. 2017, deadspin.com/michigan-state-cant-bury-its-role-in-the-largest-sex-ab-1821129797.

137-141. Mencarini, Matt. "Attorney: MSU Failed to 'Adequately Investigate' 2014 Nassar Complaint." *Lansing State Journal*, Lansing, 20 Mar. 2017, www.lansingstatejournal.com/story/news/local/2017/03/20/attorney-msu-failed-adequately-investigate-2014-nassar-complaint/99413154/.

142-145. Mencarini, Matt. "2014 Police Report Sheds Light on How Nassar Avoided Criminal Charges." *Lansing State Journal*, Lansing State Journal, 26 Jan. 2018, www.lansingstatejournal.com/story/news/local/2018/01/26/larry-nassar-michigan-state-investigation/1064914001/.

146-150. Mencarini, Matt. "Larry Nassar: 2014 Police Report Sheds Light on How He Avoided Criminal Charges." *USA Today*, Gannett Satellite Information Network, 26 Jan. 2018, www.usatoday.com/story/news/nation-now/2018/01/26/larry-nassar-michigan-state-university-investigation/1069151001/.

151. Mencarini, Matt. "2014 Police Report Sheds Light on How Nassar
Avoided Criminal Charges." *Lansing State Journal*, Lansing State
Journal, 26 Jan. 2018,
www.lansingstatejournal.com/story/news/local/2018/01/26/larry-
nassar-michigan-state-investigation/1064914001/.

152. Connor, Tracy. "FBI Says Gymnastics Doctor Larry Nassar Recorded
Abuse on Go Pro." *NBCNews.com*, NBCUniversal News Group,
21 Dec. 2016, www.nbcnews.com/news/us-news/gymnastics-
doctor-larry-nassar-hit-new-sex-abuse-claim-n698741.

153,154. "Working to Reform Marijuana Laws." *The National
Organization for the Reform of Marijuana Laws*,
norml.org/laws/item/michigan-penalties-2.

155. O'Connor, Madison. "Nassar to Be Sentenced for Child Pornography
Charges This Week." *The State News*, 6 Dec. 2017,
statenews.com/article/2017/12/nassar-federal-sentencing-preview.

156. "Drug Possession With Intent to Distribute." *FreeAdvice*, criminal-
law.freeadvice.com/criminal-
law/drug_crimes/defense_caught.htm.

157-168. Wells, Kate. "MSU Student: Gymnastics Team Told Not to Talk
to Police about Alleged Abuse." *Michigan Radio*,
michiganradio.org/post/msu-student-gymnastics-team-told-not-
talk-police-about-alleged-abuse.

169. "Larry Nassar Has Been Accused of Abuse by 265 People." *Time*,
Time, time.com/5127119/larry-nassar-how-many-victims/.

170-196. Ley, Bob and Jeremy Schaap. *"Is Anyone Listening? Crisis at Michigan State.ESPN E:60*, 28 Jan. 2017, www.espn.com/watch/player?id=3281832.

197. Toppo, Greg. "What You Need to Know about Betsy DeVos." *USA Today*, Gannett Satellite Information Network, 7 Feb. 2017, www.usatoday.com/story/news/2017/02/07/facts-about-education-secretary-betsy-devos/97605238/.

198-213. Ley, Bob and Jeremy Schaap. *"Is Anyone Listening? Crisis at Michigan State.ESPN E:60*, 28 Jan. 2017, www.espn.com/watch/player?id=3281832.

214. United States. Dept. of Health and Human Services. Office on Trafficking In Persons. *Fact Sheet: Human Trafficking*. 2017. Web. 21 November 2017.

215. Messer, Olivia. "Ex-Baylor Coach Caught Lying Again About Murdered Player." *The Daily Beast*, The Daily Beast Company, 12 Mar. 2017, www.thedailybeast.com/ex-baylor-coach-caught-lying-again-about-murdered-player.

216. Schnitzer, Kyle. "Disgraced Coach: Murdered Baylor Player Sold Drugs, Was 'the Worst'." *New York Post*, New York Post, 13 Mar. 2017, nypost.com/2017/03/13/disgraced-coach-murdered-baylor-player-sold-drugs-was-the-worst/

217. "Stanton Steps Down As Athletic Director." *Media Communications | Baylor University*, 19 Aug. 2003, www.baylor.edu/mediacommunications/news.php/news.php?action=story&story=5415.

218. Press, Houston. "Art Briles Hired by Baylor." *Houston Press*, 24
      May 2016, www.houstonpress.com/news/art-briles-hired-by-
      baylor-6400291.

219. Woods, Tim & Tribune-Herald staff. "Ken Starr Named President of
     Baylor University." *WacoTrib.com*, 16 Feb. 2010,
     www.wacotrib.com/news/ken-starr-named-president-of-baylor-
     university/article_34435a28-62a2-5676-b3b6-92b623fc16e9.html.

220. Barkham, Patrick. "Clinton Impeachment Timeline." *The Guardian*,
     Guardian News and Media, 18 Nov. 1998,
     www.theguardian.com/world/1998/nov/18/clinton.usa.

221,222. Dennis, Regina. "Starr Pushed for Lighter Sentence for
     Convicted Va. Child Molester." *WacoTrib.com*, 12 Dec. 2013,
     www.wacotrib.com/news/higher_education/starr-pushed-for-
     lighter-sentence-for-convicted-va-child-
     molester/article_56d5c672-febc-5dac-9165-83c41758ce44.html.

223. Beckford, Martin. "80% Of Women Don't Report Rape or Sexual
     Assault, Survey Claims." *The Telegraph*, Telegraph Media Group,
     12 Mar. 2012,
     www.telegraph.co.uk/news/uknews/crime/9134799/Sexual-assault-
     survey-80-of-women-dont-report-rape-or-sexual-assault-survey-
     claims.html.

224. "The 8 Biggest Recent Revelations in Baylor's Sexual Assault
     Scandal." *SportsDay*, 24 May 2017,
     sportsday.dallasnews.com/college-
     sports/collegesports/2017/05/24/5-biggest-recent-revelations-
     baylors-sexual-assault-scandal

225. "Timeline: Baylor Sexual Assault Controversy." *WacoTrib.com*, 1 Jan. 2017, www.wacotrib.com/news/higher_education/timeline-baylor-sexual-assault-controversy/article_abf21ab8-2267-51bf-84d8-6268f4222af0.html.

226. "Patty Crawford Timeline." Baylor University . https://www.baylor.edu/thefacts/doc.php/275685.pdf

227. reports, From staff. "Baylor Inquiry into Handling of Sex Assault Finished, School to Enlist Outside Investigator." *WacoTrib.com*, 28 Aug. 2015, www.wacotrib.com/sports/baylor/football/baylor-inquiry-into-handling-of-sex-assault-finished-school-to/article_f42b148a-471a-5ed2-8015-fcb07265544f.html.

228. News, CBS. "Woman Who Led Baylor Sex Assault Investigation Speaks out after Resigning." *CBS News*, CBS Interactive, 5 Oct. 2016, www.cbsnews.com/news/baylor-university-sexual-assault-scandal-title-ix-coordinator-patty-crawford-resigns/.

229. Ericksen, Phillip. "Former Title IX Chief Crawford Had Resources, Support, Baylor Says." *WacoTrib.com*, 1 Nov. 2016, www.wacotrib.com/news/higher_education/former-title-ix-chief-crawford-had-resources-support-baylor-says/article_5135e3cb-6188-576e-b851-5d0625ac278c.html.

230,231 "Ex-Baylor Title IX Boss Speaks out after Resigning." *SI.com*, www.si.com/college-football/2016/10/05/baylor-title-ix-patty-crawford-cbs-morning-interview.

232. "The 8 Biggest Recent Revelations in Baylor's Sexual Assault Scandal." *SportsDay*, 24 May 2017, sportsday.dallasnews.com/college-sports/collegesports/2017/05/24/5-biggest-recent-revelations-baylors-sexual-assault-scandal

233. *Title Ix Investigator Salary*, www.payscale.com/research/US/Job=Title_Ix_Investigator/Salary.

234. "Timeline: Baylor Sexual Assault Controversy." *WacoTrib.com*, 1 Jan. 2017, www.wacotrib.com/news/higher_education/timeline-baylor-sexual-assault-controversy/article_abf21ab8-2267-51bf-84d8-6268f4222af0.html.

235. Ericksen, Phillip. "Baylor, Alleged Gang Rape Victim Reach Settlement in Title IX Suit." *WacoTrib.com*, 5 Sept. 2017, www.wacotrib.com/news/courts_and_trials/baylor-alleged-gang-rape-victim-reach-settlement-in-title-ix/article_da7a083d-42be-570d-adb8-a1a87d4681b6.html.

236. Witherspoon, Tommy. "Baylor Hires Philadelphia Firm to Investigate Sexual Assault Cases." *WacoTrib.com*, 2 Sept. 2015, www.wacotrib.com/news/higher_education/baylor-hires-philadelphia-firm-to-investigate-sexual-assault-cases/article_e1db4a63-aa27-533a-a4f5-e9ca4f71c5ce.html.

237. Ericksen, Phillip. "Baylor Officials Not Commenting as Regents Receive Report on Rape." *WacoTrib.com*, 13 May 2016, www.wacotrib.com/news/higher_education/baylor-officials-not-commenting-as-regents-receive-report-on-rape/article_5a7b31fc-ff63-5d1d-aadd-0dc06be98f00.html

238. Ericksen, Phillip. "Starr Knew of Violence Allegations against Chafin, Title IX Lawsuit Plaintiff Says." *WacoTrib.com*, 27 July 2017, www.wacotrib.com/news/courts_and_trials/starr-knew-of-violence-allegations-against-chafin-title-ix-lawsuit/article_b91704b6-1e97-5fd8-b7c0-c7ae23fa765e.html

239-241. Ericksen, Phillip. "Baylor Officials Not Commenting as Regents Receive Report on Rape." *WacoTrib.com*, 13 May 2016, www.wacotrib.com/news/higher_education/baylor-officials-not-commenting-as-regents-receive-report-on-rape/article_5a7b31fc-ff63-5d1d-aadd-0dc06be98f00.html

242. Smith, J.B. "Report Shows Systemic Failure in Sex Crime Response at Baylor." *WacoTrib.com*, 26 May 2016, www.wacotrib.com/news/higher_education/report-shows-systemic-failure-in-sex-crime-response-at-baylor/article_432b820a-6e64-5864-92c2-f3081f020384.html

243. Anderson, Nick. "Kenneth Starr Tells ESPN He Has Resigned as Chancellor of Baylor U." *The Washington Post*, WP Company, 1 June 2016, www.washingtonpost.com/news/grade-point/wp/2016/06/01/report-kenneth-starr-resigns-as-chancellor-at-baylor-university/?utm_term=.d8f3c6ef9dbe.

244. Whitaker, Bill. "After Resigning as Chancellor, Starr Says Baylor Should Release Full Findings from Pepper Hamilton." *WacoTrib.com*, 1 June 2016, www.wacotrib.com/news/higher_education/after-resigning-as-chancellor-starr-says-baylor-should-release-full/article_64a680ad-63d1-5d60-b3bb-040b4b745166.html.

245. Ericksen, Phillip. "Baylor Officials Not Commenting as Regents Receive Report on Rape." *WacoTrib.com*, 13 May 2016, www.wacotrib.com/news/higher_education/baylor-officials-not-commenting-as-regents-receive-report-on-rape/article_5a7b31fc-ff63-5d1d-aadd-0dc06be98f00.html

246. Jane Doe 1, Jane Doe 2, Jane Doe 3, Jane Doe 4, Jane Doe 5, Jane Doe 6 vs. Baylor University. United States District Court For The Western District of Texas Waco Division. 14 June 2017. N.p., n.d. Web. https://bloximages.chicago2.vip.townnews.com/wacotrib.com/content/tncms/assets/v3/editorial/c/1b/c1b86d73-45a4-5a29-8536-cc3ecdcf661f/5942edd3a8e9e.pdf.pdf

247-249. Ericksen, Phillip. "Baylor Interim President Garland Sets Sights on Implementing Pepper Hamilton Recommendations." *WacoTrib.com*, 6 June 2016, www.wacotrib.com/news/higher_education/baylor-interim-president-garland-sets-sights-on-implementing-pepper-hamilton/article_f3e31f27-c9b7-569e-9af8-cd6fb4b66d8f.html.

250. Smith, J.B. "Report Shows Systemic Failure in Sex Crime Response at Baylor." *WacoTrib.com*, 26 May 2016, www.wacotrib.com/news/higher_education/report-shows-systemic-failure-in-sex-crime-response-at-baylor/article_432b820a-6e64-5864-92c2-f3081f020384.html.

251. Ap. "Ken Starr Makes Announcement after Being Ousted as Baylor President." *CBS News*, CBS Interactive, 1 June 2016, www.cbsnews.com/news/ken-starr-baylor-university-president-resigns-college-chancellor-sex-assault-scandal/.

252. Kercheval, Ben. "Baylor Fires Coach Art Briles amid Football Sexual Assault Investigation." *CBSSports.com*, 26 May 2016, www.cbssports.com/college-football/news/reports-baylor-fires-coach-art-briles-amid-football-program-sexual-assault-investigation/

253. "Timeline: Baylor Sexual Assault Controversy." *WacoTrib.com*, 1 Jan. 2017, www.wacotrib.com/news/higher_education/timeline-baylor-sexual-assault-controversy/article_abf21ab8-2267-51bf-84d8-6268f4222af0.html.

254,255 Lavigne, Paula. "Fired Coach Art Briles Says Baylor Using Him as Scapegoat." *ESPN*, ESPN Internet Ventures, 16 June 2016, www.espn.com/college-football/story/_/id/16257188/fired-coach-art-briles-accuses-baylor-university-wrongful-termination.

256. Ericksen, Phillip. "Crawford Says Baylor Leadership Drove Discriminatory Culture." *WacoTrib.com*, 1 Nov. 2016, www.wacotrib.com/news/higher_education/crawford-says-baylor-leadership-drove-discriminatory-culture/article_b3df9edd-2386-5ecb-bd05-45087f80c70a.html.

257. Ericksen, Phillip. "Baylor Title IX Coordinator Resigns, School Says She Demanded Movie Rights in Mediation." *WacoTrib.com*, 4 Oct. 2016, www.wacotrib.com/news/higher_education/baylor-title-ix-coordinator-resigns-school-says-she-demanded-movie/article_e6a3d8b4-3e55-5c02-8d41-a9d6c3d681fe.html.

258,259 Lavigne, Paula. "Former Baylor Title IX Coordinator Says School Stood in Her Way." *ESPN*, ESPN Internet Ventures, 5 Oct. 2016, www.espn.com/college-football/story/_/id/17720930/former-baylor-title-ix-coordinator-patty-crawford-says-school-hindered-ability-do-job

260. Ericksen, Phillip. "Baylor Title IX Coordinator Resigns, School Says She Demanded Movie Rights in Mediation." *WacoTrib.com*, 4 Oct. 2016, www.wacotrib.com/news/higher_education/baylor-title-ix-coordinator-resigns-school-says-she-demanded-movie/article_e6a3d8b4-3e55-5c02-8d41-a9d6c3d681fe.html.

261. "Timeline: Baylor Sexual Assault Controversy." *WacoTrib.com*, 1 Jan. 2017, www.wacotrib.com/news/higher_education/timeline-baylor-sexual-assault-controversy/article_abf21ab8-2267-51bf-84d8-6268f4222af0.html.

262. News, CBS. "Woman Who Led Baylor Sex Assault Investigation Speaks out after Resigning." *CBS News*, CBS Interactive, 5 Oct. 2016, www.cbsnews.com/news/baylor-university-sexual-assault-scandal-title-ix-coordinator-patty-crawford-resigns/.

263. Werner, John. "Baylor Title IX Coordinator Sees Encouraging Signs." *WacoTrib.com*, 4 Sept. 2015, www.wacotrib.com/news/higher_education/baylor-title-ix-coordinator-sees-encouraging-signs/article_7a80b2b1-4b7a-5f57-a1f9-e3557a4559f0.html.

264-266. "Timeline: Baylor Sexual Assault Controversy." *WacoTrib.com*, 1 Jan. 2017, www.wacotrib.com/news/higher_education/timeline-baylor-sexual-assault-controversy/article_abf21ab8-2267-51bf-84d8-6268f4222af0.html.

267. Ericksen, Phillip. "Briles Alleges Baylor Lawyers Were Negligent, Claims Wrongful Termination." *WacoTrib.com*, 16 June 2016, www.wacotrib.com/news/higher_education/briles-alleges-baylor-lawyers-were-negligent-claims-wrongful-termination/article_2bb92af2-33e7-11e6-a225-4fe17d75c437.html.

268. "Damning Texts between Ex-Baylor Coach Briles, Other Officials Revealed in New Court Records." *Dallas News*, 2 Feb. 2017, www.dallasnews.com/news/baylor/2017/02/02/ex-baylor-coach-art-briles-officials-tried-hide-misconduct-football-players-court-record-shows#_ga=2.146724532.1252374146.1517295296-2038915578.1517295296.

269,270. "Kalyn Story." *The Baylor Lariat*, 31 Oct. 2016, baylorlariat.com/2016/10/31/regents-address-sexual-assault-mishandelings-at-baylor/. http://baylorlariat.com/2016/10/31/regents-address-sexual-assault-mishandelings-at-baylor/

271. Ericksen, Phillip. "Crawford Says Baylor Leadership Drove Discriminatory Culture." *WacoTrib.com*, 1 Nov. 2016, www.wacotrib.com/news/higher_education/crawford-says-baylor-leadership-drove-discriminatory-culture/article_b3df9edd-2386-5ecb-bd05-45087f80c70a.html.

272. Redford, Patrick. "New Report Details How Baylor Suppressed Reports Of Sexual Assault." *Deadspin*, Deadspin.com, 2 Nov. 2016, deadspin.com/new-report-details-how-baylor-suppressed-reports-of-sex-1788471921.

273. "About." *NCAA.org - The Official Site of the NCAA*, www.ncaa.org/about.

274. Jenkins, Sally. "Perspective | If NCAA Ignores Baylor Rape Scandal, It Deserves the Death Penalty." *The Washington Post*, WP Company, 31 Jan. 2017, www.washingtonpost.com/sports/colleges/if-ncaa-ignores-baylor-rape-scandal-it-deserves-the-death-penalty/2017/01/31/e597cbb4-e7b9-11e6-bf6f-301b6b443624_story.html?utm_term=.83bbdae37378.

275. "Timeline: Baylor Sexual Assault Controversy." *WacoTrib.com*, 1 Jan. 2017, www.wacotrib.com/news/higher_education/timeline-baylor-sexual-assault-controversy/article_abf21ab8-2267-51bf-84d8-6268f4222af0.html.

276. "Board of Regents 2017-2018." *Board of Regents | Baylor University*, www.baylor.edu/boardofregents/index.php?id=937243.

277. "Timeline: Baylor Sexual Assault Controversy." *WacoTrib.com*, 1 Jan. 2017, www.wacotrib.com/news/higher_education/timeline-baylor-sexual-assault-controversy/article_abf21ab8-2267-51bf-84d8-6268f4222af0.html.

278. "Timeline: Baylor Sexual Assault Controversy." *WacoTrib.com*, 1 Jan. 2017, www.wacotrib.com/news/higher_education/timeline-baylor-sexual-assault-controversy/article_abf21ab8-2267-51bf-84d8-6268f4222af0.html.

279. "Forcing Baylor University Regents into the Sunlight: Q&A with Bears for Leadership Reform." *WacoTrib.com*, 20 Nov. 2016, www.wacotrib.com/opinion/interviews/forcing-baylor-university-regents-into-the-sunlight-q-a-with/article_421afc1b-d307-5486-a627-ee2c692b32ac.html.

280,281. Ericksen, Phillip. "Baylor Regents Shed Light on Pepper Hamilton Review with Faculty, Staff." *WacoTrib.com*, 2 Dec. 2016, www.wacotrib.com/news/higher_education/baylor-regents-shed-light-on-pepper-hamilton-review-with-faculty/article_7a3fa5a1-9ba9-5ad3-b9f0-84657e8be856.html.

282. "Timeline: Baylor Sexual Assault Controversy." *WacoTrib.com*, 1 Jan. 2017, www.wacotrib.com/news/higher_education/timeline-baylor-sexual-assault-controversy/article_abf21ab8-2267-51bf-84d8-6268f4222af0.html.

283. "BAYLOR UNIVERSITY REPORT OF EXTERNAL AND INDEPENDENT REVIEW." Pepper and Hamilton, LLP, 13 May 2016.
https://www.baylor.edu/thefacts/doc.php/266597.pdf

284. "BAYLOR UNIVERSITY BOARD OF REGENTS FINDINGS OF FACT." Baylor University Board of Regents, 26 May 2016.
https://www.baylor.edu/thefacts/doc.php/266596.pdf

285,286. "Timeline: Baylor Sexual Assault Controversy." *WacoTrib.com*, 1 Jan. 2017, www.wacotrib.com/news/higher_education/timeline-baylor-sexual-assault-controversy/article_abf21ab8-2267-51bf-84d8-6268f4222af0.html.

287. Watkins, Matthew. "Baylor Ordered to Turn over Records from Sexual Assault Investigation." *The Texas Tribune*, Texas Tribune, 11 Aug. 2017, www.texastribune.org/2017/08/11/baylor-ordered-turn-over-documents-pepper-hamilton-report/.

288. Ericksen, Phillip. Ericksen, Phillip. "Big 12 Asks Baylor to Turn over Full Pepper Hamilton Report." *WacoTrib.com*, 22 June 2016, http://www.wacotrib.com/news/higher_education/big-asks-baylor-to-turn-over-full-pepper-hamilton-report/article_f7251ce7-c57a-5ba8-8ff0-98f5502c2fc9.html289. Ericksen, Phillip. "Baylor Donors Call for Independent Investigation of Regents." *WacoTrib.com*, 5 Dec. 2016, www.wacotrib.com/news/higher_education/baylor-donors-call-for-independent-investigation-of-regents/article_b1351334-a00d-52db-a057-c3929f87f87a.html.

290,291. Bieler, Des. "Art Briles Suing Baylor Officials for Accusing Him of Covering up Sexual Assaults." *The Washington Post*, WP Company, 8 Dec. 2016, www.washingtonpost.com/news/early-lead/wp/2016/12/08/art-briles-suing-baylor-for-accusing-him-of-covering-up-sexual-assaults/?utm_term=.21eb56e6541a.

292. "Timeline: Baylor Sexual Assault Controversy." *WacoTrib.com*, 1 Jan. 2017, www.wacotrib.com/news/higher_education/timeline-baylor-sexual-assault-controversy/article_abf21ab8-2267-51bf-84d8-6268f4222af0.html.

293. Ericksen, Phillip. "Baylor Regents, Administrator Deny Making False Statements amid Scandal." *WacoTrib.com*, 12 Jan. 2017, www.wacotrib.com/news/higher_education/baylor-regents-administrator-deny-making-false-statements-amid-scandal/article_e3149778-be30-5f16-bda1-892ade8014e1.html.

294-296. "Timeline: Baylor Sexual Assault Controversy." *WacoTrib.com*, 1 Jan. 2017, www.wacotrib.com/news/higher_education/timeline-baylor-sexual-assault-controversy/article_abf21ab8-2267-51bf-84d8-6268f4222af0.html.

297. Ericksen, Phillip. "Pepper Hamilton Denies Claims of Former Baylor Athletics Staffer Hill." *WacoTrib.com*, 23 Jan. 2017, www.wacotrib.com/news/courts_and_trials/pepper-hamilton-denies-claims-of-former-baylor-athletics-staffer-hill/article_03f83481-e676-58de-bd2a-11c77e43a894.html.

298. "New Baylor Lawsuit Alleges 52 Rapes by Football Players in 4 Years, 'Show 'Em a Good Time' Culture." *Dallas News*, 27 Jan. 2017, www.dallasnews.com/news/baylor/2017/01/27/new-baylor-lawsuit-describes-show-em-good-time-culture-cites-52-rapes-football-players-4-years.

299. "Train." *Urban Dictionary*, www.urbandictionary.com/define.php?term=train.

300. Hoppa, Kristin, and Phillip Ericksen. "New Title IX Lawsuit Alleges Culture of Sexual Violence at Baylor." *WacoTrib.com*, 27 Jan. 2017, www.wacotrib.com/news/courts_and_trials/new-title-ix-lawsuit-alleges-culture-of-sexual-violence-at/article_5fdb812d-e0d1-5dae-9c07-519380d305f7.html.

301. Zahn, Harry. "Baylor and Waco Police Buried Reports of Sexual Assaults, Report Says." *PBS*, Public Broadcasting Service, 2 Nov. 2016, www.pbs.org/newshour/nation/baylor-waco-police-sexual-assault-reports.

302. Colin Shillinglaw vs. Baylor University, Dr. David E. Garland in His Official Capacity as Interim President Of Baylor University, Reagan Ramsower, James Cary Gray, Ronald D. Murff, David H. Harper, Dr. Dennis R. Wiles and Pepper Hamilton, L.L.P. *116th Judicial District; 5th Court of Appeals*. 22 June 2017. N.p., n.d. Web. http://bloximages.chicago2.vip.townnews.com/wacotrib.com/content/tncms/assets/v3/editorial/b/ac/bacc361a-e9b5-11e6-ad87-5fd2d6e674d8/5893e6dfbdcf3.pdf.pdf

303. Werner, John. "Big 12 to Withhold Revenue to Baylor Pending Review." *WacoTrib.com*, 8 Feb. 2017, www.wacotrib.com/news/higher_education/big-to-withhold-revenue-to-baylor-pending-review/article_143b05d3-763c-52f5-8d2b-6c694c6ea8df.html.

304. Ericksen, Phillip. "Baylor Launches New Board Website, Releases Friday Agenda." *WacoTrib.com*, 13 Feb. 2017, www.wacotrib.com/news/higher_education/baylor-launches-new-board-website-releases-friday-agenda/article_d958f991-340d-566f-8744-036eed8d53a7.html.

305. Ericksen, Phillip. "Baylor Launches New Board Website, Releases Friday Agenda." *WacoTrib.com*, 13 Feb. 2017, www.wacotrib.com/news/higher_education/baylor-launches-new-board-website-releases-friday-agenda/article_d958f991-340d-566f-8744-036eed8d53a7.html.

306. Zagger, Zachary. "Jane Does Demand Pepper Hamilton's Baylor Report Docs - Law360." *Law360 - The Newswire for Business Lawyers*, www.law360.com/articles/907497/jane-does-demand-pepper-hamilton-s-baylor-report-docs.

307. Watkins, Matthew. "Texas Rangers Investigating Sexual Assault Scandal at Baylor." *The Texas Tribune*, Texas Tribune, 1 Mar. 2017, www.texastribune.org/2017/03/01/texas-rangers-investigating-sexual-assault-scandal-baylor/.

308. "Aggressive Campus Anti-Rape Laws Proposed for Texas Colleges in Wake of Baylor Scandal." *Dallas News*, 21 Feb. 2017, www.dallasnews.com/news/higher-education/2017/02/21/school-staffcould-fined-jailed-aggressive-push-fight-campus-rape-spurred-baylor-scandal.

309,310. "Timeline: Baylor Sexual Assault Controversy." *WacoTrib.com*, 1 Jan. 2017, www.wacotrib.com/news/higher_education/timeline-baylor-sexual-assault-controversy/article_abf21ab8-2267-51bf-84d8-6268f4222af0.html.

311. "Baylor Scandal Inspires Raft of Texas Campus Assault Bills." *Amarillo.com*, 5 Apr. 2017, amarillo.com/texas-news/news/crime-and-courts/2017-04-05/baylor-scandal-inspires-raft-texas-campus-assault-bills.

312. Ericksen, Phillip. "Baylor Settles 1 of 6 Title IX Lawsuits."
WacoTrib.com, 6 July 2017,
www.wacotrib.com/news/courts_and_trials/baylor-settles-of-title-
ix-lawsuits/article_1dff70b0-10ca-522b-bc94-4244b0e84c5e.html.

313. "Baylor Settles Lawsuit with Woman Who Alleged Rape." *SI.com*,
www.si.com/college-football/2017/07/07/baylor-sexual-assault-
probe-lawsuit.

314. "Baylor Seminary Student Arrested for Sexual Assault of Child."
KCEN, 28 Feb. 2017, www.kcentv.com/article/news/local/baylor-
seminary-student-arrested-for-sexual-assault-of-child/500-
416208875.

315. "Timeline: Baylor Sexual Assault Controversy." *WacoTrib.com*, 1
Jan. 2017, www.wacotrib.com/news/higher_education/timeline-
baylor-sexual-assault-controversy/article_abf21ab8-2267-51bf-
84d8-6268f4222af0.html.316,317. Ericksen, Phillip. "In Emails,
Then-Baylor Regent Calls Students Suspected of Drinking
'Perverted Little Tarts'." *WacoTrib.com*, 1 July 2017,
www.wacotrib.com/news/courts_and_trials/in-emails-then-baylor-
regent-calls-students-suspected-of-drinking/article_c88a8812-72ef-
5301-b35e-8d845e8dbdc6.html.

318. Conlon, Shelly. "5th U.S. Circuit Court of Appeals Denies Baylor's
Attempt to Block Release of Student Records in Title IX Suit."
WacoTrib.com, 12 Dec. 2017,
www.wacotrib.com/news/higher_education/th-u-s-circuit-court-of-
appeals-denies-baylor-s/article_59657c47-94b4-519e-8912-
9fde5e814adf.html.

319. "Timeline: Baylor Sexual Assault Controversy." *WacoTrib.com*, 1 Jan. 2017, www.wacotrib.com/news/higher_education/timeline-baylor-sexual-assault-controversy/article_abf21ab8-2267-51bf-84d8-6268f4222af0.html.

320. Ericksen, Phillip. "Baylor Ordered to Release 'Original' Sexual Assault Reports since 2003." *WacoTrib.com*, 27 July 2017, www.wacotrib.com/news/courts_and_trials/baylor-ordered-to-release-original-sexual-assault-reports-since/article_0052b4af-47dc-5078-b130-428f907246e3.html.

321,322. Witherspoon, Tommy. "Judge Umpires Discovery Disputes in Baylor-Jane Doe Lawsuit." *WacoTrib.com*, 28 July 2017, www.wacotrib.com/news/courts_and_trials/judge-umpires-discovery-disputes-in-baylor-jane-doe-lawsuit/article_afd0b867-b52d-5b9a-9d24-27f087e34fe9.html.

323. Watkins, Matthew. "Baylor Ordered to Turn over Records from Sexual Assault Investigation." *The Texas Tribune*, Texas Tribune, 11 Aug. 2017, www.texastribune.org/2017/08/11/baylor-ordered-turn-over-documents-pepper-hamilton-report/.

324. Ericksen, Phillip. "Baylor Ordered to Produce Long-Secretive Pepper Hamilton Information in Title IX Suit." *WacoTrib.com*, 11 Aug. 2017, www.wacotrib.com/news/courts_and_trials/baylor-ordered-to-produce-long-secretive-pepper-hamilton-information-in/article_e48e5d14-082e-5279-92f0-7fa73a5db207.html.

325,326. Wral. "Coastal Carolina Cheerleading Team Suspended amid Prostitution Allegations." *WRAL.com*, 4 Apr. 2017, www.wral.com/ccu-cheerleading-team-suspended-cheerleader-says-anonymous-letter-alleged-prostitution-misconduct/16625626/.

327. Havis, Michael. "Entire Cheerleader Squad SUSPENDED in Prostitute Row as Cops Question Girls." *Dailystar.co.uk*, Daily Star, 1 Apr. 2017, www.dailystar.co.uk/news/latest-news/602003/cheerleader-squad-prostitution-scandal-coastal-carolina-university-ccu-usa.

328. Duffy, Tyler. "Coastal Carolina Suspended Cheerleading Team After Anonymous Letter Accused Team of Prostitution." *The Big Lead*, 1 Apr. 2017, thebiglead.com/2017/03/31/coastal-carolina-suspended-cheerleading-team-after-anonymous-letter-accused-team-of-prostitution/.

329-332. Wral. "Coastal Carolina Cheerleading Team Suspended amid Prostitution Allegations." *WRAL.com*, 4 Apr. 2017, www.wral.com/ccu-cheerleading-team-suspended-cheerleader-says-anonymous-letter-alleged-prostitution-misconduct/16625626/.

333. Speaks, Ian Cross Sage. "CCU Cheerleading Team Suspended; Cheerleader Says Anonymous Letter Alleged Prostitution, Misconduct." *WMBF News - Grand Strand, Pee Dee News, First Alert Weather - WMBFNews.com, Myrtle Beach/Florence SC, Weather*, 30 Mar. 2017, www.wmbfnews.com/story/35034543/ccu-cheerleading-team-suspended-cheerleader-says-anonymous-letter-alleged-prostitution-misconduct.

334. Harris, Sara. "Coastal Carolina Cheerleaders Suspended amid Prostitution Allegations, Report Says." *Sporting News*, 31 Mar. 2017, www.sportingnews.com/other-sports/news/suspended-coastal-carolina-cheerleading-team-alleged-prostitution-wmbf/vove76bmdoj21b7smaq1d45cp.

335-338. Miller, Joshua Rhett. "Turns out These Cheerleaders Were 'Sugar Babies,' Not Prostitutes." *New York Post*, New York Post, 7 Apr. 2017, nypost.com/2017/04/07/how-these-suspended-cheerleaders-cashed-in-on-their-looks/.

339-341. Boschult, Christian. "CCU Cheerleaders Were Paid up to $1,500 for Dates, According to Investigation." *Thestate*, The State, www.thestate.com/news/state/south-carolina/article143169714.html.

342. Miller, Joshua Rhett. "Turns out These Cheerleaders Were 'Sugar Babies,' Not Prostitutes." *New York Post*, New York Post, 7 Apr. 2017, nypost.com/2017/04/07/how-these-suspended-cheerleaders-cashed-in-on-their-looks/.

343. "FBI Brings Armageddon to College Basketball, and It's Just the Tip of the Iceberg." *Yahoo! Sports*, Yahoo!, sports.yahoo.com/fbi-brings-armageddon-college-basketball-just-tip-iceberg-184524346.html

344,355. "U.S. Attorney Announces The Arrest Of 10 Individuals, Including Four Division I Coaches, For College Basketball Fraud And Corruption Schemes." *The United States Department of Justice*, 26 Sept. 2017, www.justice.gov/usao-sdny/pr/us-attorney-announces-arrest-10-individuals-including-four-division-i-coaches-college.

346. Heitner, Darren. "Federal Prosecutors Unveil Sweeping Bribery Case Involving Adidas, College Basketball Coaches." *Forbes*, Forbes Magazine, 26 Sept. 2017, www.forbes.com/sites/darrenheitner/2017/09/26/us-attorney-explains-charges-of-fraud-and-corruption-against-chuck-person-and-adidas-exec/#74a49d7d69f9.

347. Marcum, Jason. "More Damning Evidence of Rick Pitino Paying Players." *A Sea Of Blue*, A Sea Of Blue, 8 Nov. 2017, www.aseaofblue.com/2017/11/8/16625810/ncaa-basketball-scandal-damning-evidence-rick-pitino-paying-players.

348. Zeigler, Mark. "Indictments Expose 'Dark Underbelly of College Basketball'." *Sandiegouniontribune.com*, 27 Sept. 2017, www.sandiegouniontribune.com/sports/aztecs/sd-sp-zeigler-college-basketball-20170926-story.html.

349. Marcum, Jason. "More Damning Evidence of Rick Pitino Paying Players." *A Sea Of Blue*, A Sea Of Blue, 8 Nov. 2017, www.aseaofblue.com/2017/11/8/16625810/ncaa-basketball-scandal-damning-evidence-rick-pitino-paying-players.

350. "FBI Brings Armageddon to College Basketball, and It's Just the Tip of the Iceberg." *Yahoo! Sports*, Yahoo!, sports.yahoo.com/fbi-brings-armageddon-college-basketball-just-tip-iceberg-184524346.html.

351. Brockington, Ariana. "NCAA Suspends Louisville Basketball Coach Rick Pitino in Escort Scandal." *NBCNews.com*, NBCUniversal News Group, 15 June 2017, www.nbcnews.com/news/us-news/ncaa-suspends-louisville-basketball-coach-rick-pitino-escort-scandal-n773031.

352. Riley, Jason. "REPORT: U of L Player Told NCAA That an Assistant Coach Blamed Bad Practice on 'Strippers'." *Home - WDRB 41 Louisville News*, 15 June 2017, www.wdrb.com/story/35675621/report-u-of-l-player-told-ncaa-that-an-assistant-coach-blamed-bad-practice-on-strippers.

353-355. Barr, John. "Source: Louisville Recruits Told NCAA about Sex, Stripper Parties." *ESPN*, ESPN Internet Ventures, 13 Mar. 2016, www.espn.com/espn/otl/story/_/id/14951432/three-former-louisville-basketball-recruits-told-ncaa-investigators-attended-stripper-parties-had-sex-them.

356. "Former Escort Tells ESPN She Felt like Part of Louisville's Recruiting Team." *USA Today*, Gannett Satellite Information Network, 20 Oct. 2015, www.usatoday.com/story/sports/ncaab/2015/10/20/louisville-recruiting-escort-strippers-katina-powell/74259456/.

357. Culpepper, Chuck. "Most Call It a College Basketball Scandal. In Louisville, They Call It 'Total Armageddon.'." *The Washington Post*, WP Company, 29 Sept. 2017, www.washingtonpost.com/sports/colleges/most-call-it-a-college-basketball-scandal-in-louisville-they-call-it-total-armageddon/2017/09/29/4d355c40-a45d-11e7-ade1-76d061d56efa_story.html?utm_term=.818cfee3db15.

358. Bozich, Rick. "BOZICH | Word That Resonates in Louisville NCAA Punishment: Repugnant." *Home - WDRB 41 Louisville News*, 15 June 2017, www.wdrb.com/story/35677031/bozich-key-word-in-louisville-ncaa-punishment-repugnant.

359. Culpepper, Chuck. "Most Call It a College Basketball Scandal. In Louisville, They Call It 'Total Armageddon.'." *The Washington Post*, WP Company, 29 Sept. 2017, www.washingtonpost.com/sports/colleges/most-call-it-a-college-basketball-scandal-in-louisville-they-call-it-total-armageddon/2017/09/29/4d355c40-a45d-11e7-ade1-76d061d56efa_story.html?utm_term=.818cfee3db15

360. "Louisville Basketball Should Be given Death Penalty If Bombshell NCAA Allegations Prove True." *Yahoo! Sports*, Yahoo!, sports.yahoo.com/ncaa-needs-give-louisville-basketball-death-sentence-bombshell-allegations-prove-correct-181930063.html.

361. Levenson, Eric. "For Rick Pitino, Latest Scandal May Be One Too Many." *CNN*, Cable News Network, 27 Sept. 2017, www.cnn.com/2017/09/27/sport/rick-pitino-scandal-history/index.html.

362. Press, Associated. "Woman Faces Federal Extortion Charges." *ESPN*, ESPN Internet Ventures, 24 Apr. 2009, www.espn.com/mens-college-basketball/news/story?id=4096770.

363. "Report: Pitino Says He Paid for Abortion." *ESPN*, ESPN Internet Ventures, 12 Aug. 2009, www.espn.com/mens-college-basketball/news/story?id=4392828.

364. "Louisville Basketball Should Be given Death Penalty If Bombshell NCAA Allegations Prove True." *Yahoo! Sports*, Yahoo!, sports.yahoo.com/ncaa-needs-give-louisville-basketball-death-sentence-bombshell-allegations-prove-correct-181930063.html.

365. "Arizona Wildcats on Yahoo! Sports - News, Scores, Standings, Rumors, Fantasy Games." *Yahoo! Sports*, Yahoo!, sports.yahoo.com/ncaab/teams/aaq.

366. "Auburn Tigers on Yahoo! Sports - News, Scores, Standings, Rumors, Fantasy Games." *Yahoo! Sports*, Yahoo!, sports.yahoo.com/ncaab/teams/abb.

367. "Oklahoma State Cowboys on Yahoo! Sports - News, Scores, Standings, Rumors, Fantasy Games." *Yahoo! Sports*, Yahoo!, sports.yahoo.com/ncaab/teams/oag.

368. "USC Trojans on Yahoo! Sports - News, Scores, Standings, Rumors, Fantasy Games." *Yahoo! Sports*, Yahoo!, sports.yahoo.com/ncaab/teams/uad. https://sports.yahoo.com/ncaab/teams/uad.

369. "The Obama Administration Remade Sexual Assault Enforcement on Campus. Could Trump Unmake It?" *The Obama Administration Remade Sexual Assault Enforcement on Campus. Could Trump Unmake It? | Edify,* www.wbur.org/edify/2016/11/25/title-ix-obama-trump.

370-373. United States. Dept. of Education. Office of Civil Rights. *Dear Colleague.* 2011. Web. 4 April 2011.

374,375. Boyer, Dave. "DeVos Sworn in as Education Secretary by Pence." *The Washington Times,* The Washington Times, 7 Feb. 2017, www.washingtontimes.com/news/2017/feb/7/betsy-devos-sworn-education-secretary-pence/.

376. LoBianco, Tom, et al. "DeVos Confirmed; Vice President Casts Historic Tie-Breaking Vote." *CNN,* Cable News Network, 7 Feb. 2017, www.cnn.com/2017/02/07/politics/betsy-devos-senate-vote/index.html.

377. Saul, Stephanie, and Kate Taylor. "Betsy DeVos Reverses Obama-Era Policy on Campus Sexual Assault Investigations." *The New York Times,* The New York Times, 22 Sept. 2017, www.nytimes.com/2017/09/22/us/devos-colleges-sex-assault.html.

378. United States. Dept. of Education. Office of Civil Rights. *Dear Colleague.* 2011. Web. 4 April 2011.

379,380. United States. Dept. of Education. Office of Civil Rights. *Q&A on Campus Sexual Misconduct.* By Assistant Secretary. 2017. Web. September 2017.

381,382. Saul, Stephanie, and Kate Taylor. "Betsy DeVos Reverses Obama-Era Policy on Campus Sexual Assault Investigations." *The New York Times*, The New York Times, 22 Sept. 2017, www.nytimes.com/2017/09/22/us/devos-colleges-sex-assault.html.

383. Gersen, Jeannie Suk. "Betsy DeVos, Title IX, and the 'Both Sides' Approach to Sexual Assault." *The New Yorker*, The New Yorker, 8 Sept. 2017, www.newyorker.com/news/news-desk/betsy-devos-title-ix-and-the-both-sides-approach-to-sexual-assault.

384. Silva, Daniella. "Education Department Official Apologizes for Campus Assault Comments." *NBCNews.com*, NBCUniversal News Group, 13 July 2017, www.nbcnews.com/politics/politics-news/education-department-official-apologizes-comments-campus-sex-assaults-n782661.

385. Graves, Lucia. "The Sexual Misconduct Allegations against Donald Trump – the Full List." *The Guardian*, Guardian News and Media, www.theguardian.com/us-news/ng-interactive/2017/nov/30/donald-trump-sexual-misconduct-allegations-full-list.

386. Gersen, Jeannie Suk. "Betsy DeVos, Title IX, and the 'Both Sides' Approach to Sexual Assault." *The New Yorker*, The New Yorker, 8 Sept. 2017, www.newyorker.com/news/news-desk/betsy-devos-title-ix-and-the-both-sides-approach-to-sexual-assault.

387. "Department of Education Issues New Interim Guidance on Campus Sexual Misconduct." *Department of Education Issues New Interim Guidance on Campus Sexual Misconduct | U.S. Department of Education*, 22 Sept. 2017, www.ed.gov/news/press-releases/department-education-issues-new-interim-guidance-campus-sexual-misconduct.

388. United States. Dept. of Education. Office of Civil Rights. *Dear Colleague*. 2011. Web. 4 April 2011.

389. "Department of Education Issues New Interim Guidance on Campus Sexual Misconduct." *Department of Education Issues New Interim Guidance on Campus Sexual Misconduct | U.S. Department of Education*, 22 Sept. 2017, www.ed.gov/news/press-releases/department-education-issues-new-interim-guidance-campus-sexual-misconduct.

390. Boyer, Dave. "DeVos Sworn in as Education Secretary by Pence." *The Washington Times*, The Washington Times, 7 Feb. 2017, www.washingtontimes.com/news/2017/feb/7/betsy-devos-sworn-education-secretary-pence/.

391. Weissman, Cale Guthrie. "She Says Donald Trump Sexually Assaulted Her. Now She's Running for Office." *Fast Company*, Fast Company, 5 Feb. 2018, www.fastcompany.com/40526782/she-says-donald-trump-sexually-assaulted-her-now-shes-running-for-office.

392. Pearson, Catherine, et al. "A Running List Of The Women Who've Accused Donald Trump Of Sexual Misconduct." *The Huffington Post*, TheHuffingtonPost.com, 12 Dec. 2017, https://www.huffingtonpost.com/entry/a-running-list-of-the-women-whove-accused-donald-trump-of-sexual-misconduct_us_57ffae1fe4b0162c043a7212

393. Gersen, Jeannie Suk. "The Trump Administration's Fraught Attempt to Address Campus Sexual Assault." *The New Yorker*, The New Yorker, 17 July 2017, www.newyorker.com/news/news-desk/the-trump-administrations-fraught-attempt-to-address-campus-sexual-assault.

394. Robby, Soave. "Only 2–8% of Rape Reports Are False? Betsy DeVos Is Still Right to Fix Title IX." *Reason.com*, 11 Sept. 2017, reason.com/blog/2017/09/11/devos-campus-rape-reports-false-title-ix.

395. "Myths and Facts." *Rape Victim Advocates*, 7 June 2016, www.rapevictimadvocates.org/what-you-need-to-know/myths-and-facts/.

396. Robby, Soave. "Only 2–8% of Rape Reports Are False? Betsy DeVos Is Still Right to Fix Title IX." *Reason.com*, 11 Sept. 2017, reason.com/blog/2017/09/11/devos-campus-rape-reports-false-title-ix.

397. *About NGA*, www.nga.mil/About/Pages/Default.aspx.

398-406. Whitlock, Craig. "FBI Investigated Complaints That Bobby Knight Groped Women at U.S. Spy Agency." *The Washington Post*, WP Company, 7 July 2017, www.washingtonpost.com/investigations/fbi-investigated-complaints-that-bobby-knight-groped-women-at-us-spy-agency/2017/07/07/ee1fc318-618f-11e7-8adc-fea80e32bf47_story.html?utm_term=.dcd5bd1f22c2.

407-409. Ley, Tom. "The FBI Investigated Bobby Knight For Groping Women At A Spy Agency." *Deadspin*, Deadspin.com, 7 July 2017, deadspin.com/the-fbi-investigated-bobby-knight-for-groping-women-at-1796723422.

410. Bieler, Des. "Bobby Knight Calls Trump 'Most Prepared Man in History' to Run for President." *The Washington Post*, WP Company, 28 Apr. 2016, www.washingtonpost.com/news/early-lead/wp/2016/04/27/bobby-knight-calls-trump-most-prepared-man-in-history-to-run-for-president/?utm_term=.acad725946d8.

411. Moran, Malcolm. "Knight Is Criticized Over Rape Remark." *The New York Times*, The New York Times, 26 Apr. 1988, www.nytimes.com/1988/04/27/sports/knight-is-criticized-over-rape-remark.html.

412. "Tom Izzo Bio :: Michigan State :: Official Athletic Site." *MSUSPARTANSDOTCOM*, www.msuspartans.com/sports/m-baskbl/mtt/tom_izzo_134152.html.

413. Moskovitz, Diana. "Betsy DeVos Rolled Back Title IX Protections Two Days After Hanging Out With MSU President." *Deadspin*, Deadspin.com, 26 Jan. 2018, deadspin.com/betsy-devos-rolled-back-title-ix-protections-two-days-a-1822462475.

414. Press, Associated. "U.S. Education Secretary Betsy DeVos Says Agency Investigating Michigan State." *Lansing State Journal*, Lansing State Journal, 26 Jan. 2018, www.lansingstatejournal.com/story/news/2018/01/26/u-s-education-secretary-betsy-devos-says-agency-investigating-michigan-state/1069609001/.

415. Connor, Tracy. "In Larry Nassar Probe, Michigan Attorney General Schuette Eyes Former MSU Staffers." *NBCNews.com*, NBCUniversal News Group, 29 Jan. 2018, www.nbcnews.com/news/us-news/larry-nassar-probe-michigan-attorney-general-schuette-eyes-former-msu-n842451.

416. "Dunnings Sentenced to 1 Year in Jail, 3 Years Probation for Human Trafficking-Related Prostitution Offenses, Misconduct in Office." *AG - Dunnings Sentenced to 1 Year in Jail, 3 Years Probation for Human Trafficking-Related Prostitution Offenses, Misconduct in Office*, www.michigan.gov/ag/0,4534,7-359-82916_81983_47203-397839--m_2010_2,00.html.

417,418. News, The Detroit. "Investigators Execute Search Warrant at MSU." *Detroit News*, 2 Feb. 2018, www.detroitnews.com/story/news/local/michigan/2018/02/02/msu-investigation-search/110062122/.

419. "The Death of Daria Pionko Shows There Is No 'Safe' Way to Manage Prostitution." *New Statesman*, www.newstatesman.com/politics/feminism/2016/01/death-daria-pionko-shows-there-no-safe-way-manage-prostitution.

420. Gannon, Megan. "What Kind of Men Go to Prostitutes?" *LiveScience*, Purch, 25 Mar. 2013, www.livescience.com/28169-men-who-use-prostitutes.html.

421. Westerhoff, Nikolas. "Why Do Men Buy Sex?" *Scientific American*, 1 Oct. 2012, www.scientificamerican.com/article/why-do-men-buy-sex-2012-10-23/.

422. Shrier, Adam. "Massive Human Trafficking Sting in Texas Leads to 61 Arrests." *NY Daily News*, NEW YORK DAILY NEWS, 28 June 2016, www.nydailynews.com/news/crime/massive-human-trafficking-sting-texas-leads-61-arrests-article-1.2691718.

423. Lines, Lisa (2015). Prostitution in Thailand: Representations in Fiction and Narrative Non-Fiction. *Journal of International Women's Studies*, 16(3), 86-100. Available at: http://vc.bridgew.edu/jiws/vol16/iss3/7

424. "Sex for Sale: Why Sweden Punishes Buyers." *The Christian Science Monitor*, The Christian Science Monitor, 7 Sept. 2010, www.csmonitor.com/Commentary/Opinion/2010/0907/Sex-for-sale-Why-Sweden-punishes-buyers.

425. "American Greed." *CNBC*, CNBC, 15 Feb. 2018, www.cnbc.com/american-greed/.

426. "Edward Abbey Quotes." *BrainyQuote*, Xplore, https://www.brainyquote.com/quotes/edward_abbey_104709

427. "Sex Trafficking in the U.S.: A Closer Look at U.S. Citizen Victims." *Polaris*, 1 Mar. 2016, https://polarisproject.org/sites/default/files/us-citizen-sex-trafficking.pdf

428,429. Barr, John. "Source: Louisville Recruits Told NCAA about Sex, Stripper Parties." *ESPN*, ESPN Internet Ventures, 13 Mar. 2016, www.espn.com/espn/otl/story/_/id/14951432/three-former-louisville-basketball-recruits-told-ncaa-investigators-attended-stripper-parties-had-sex-them.

430. NCAA. NCAA Division I Baseball Recruiting Calendar. N.p.: National Collegiate Athletic Association, June 2016. PDF. http://www.ncaa.org/sites/default/files/June2016_DIBaseballCalendar_20160613.pdf

431. NCAA. "Division I Recruiting - Official - Unofficial Visits." National Collegiate Athletic Association, 29 Apr. 2016. https://www.ncaa.org/sites/default/files/DI_Recruiting_Official_Unofficial_Visits-SEMINAR_06302016.pdf

432. Barr, John. "Source: Louisville Recruits Told NCAA about Sex, Stripper Parties." *ESPN*, ESPN Internet Ventures, 13 Mar. 2016, www.espn.com/espn/otl/story/_/id/14951432/three-former-louisville-basketball-recruits-told-ncaa-investigators-attended-stripper-parties-had-sex-them.

433. *ESPN*, ESPN Internet Ventures, www.espn.com/mens-college-basketball/team/roster/_/id/97/louisville-cardinals.

434. NCAA. "Division I Recruiting - Official - Unofficial Visits."
National Collegiate Athletic Association, 29 Apr. 2016.
https://www.ncaa.org/sites/default/files/DI_Recruiting_Official_Unofficial
_Visits-SEMINAR_06302016.pdf

435, 436. 54A Judicial District 30 Judicial Circuit. *People of the State of
Michigan v Stuart Dunnings, III and Steven Dunnings.* Mar. 2016,
www.michigan.gov/documents/ag/Stuart_Dunnings-Affidavit_-
_54A_-_Dunnings_516941_7.pdf.

437. "Accommodation | About USA." *Rough Guides,*
www.roughguides.com/destinations/north-
america/usa/accommodation/.

438-441. 54A Judicial District 30 Judicial Circuit. *People of the State of
Michigan v Stuart Dunnings, III and Steven Dunnings.* Mar. 2016,
www.michigan.gov/documents/ag/Stuart_Dunnings-Affidavit_-
_54A_-_Dunnings_516941_7.pdf.

442. Abuse, National Institute on Drug. "How Long Does Drug Addiction
Treatment Usually Last?" *NIDA,*
www.drugabuse.gov/publications/principles-drug-addiction-
treatment-research-based-guide-third-edition/frequently-asked-
questions/how-long-does-drug-addiction-treatment.

443-450. 54A Judicial District 30 Judicial Circuit. *People of the State of
Michigan v Stuart Dunnings, III and Steven Dunnings.* Mar. 2016,
www.michigan.gov/documents/ag/Stuart_Dunnings-Affidavit_-
_54A_-_Dunnings_516941_7.pdf.

451. P., Lynn. "WEST LANSING FAIRFIELD INN." *Lansing MI 810 Delta Commerce 48917*, 13 Feb. 2017, www.hotelplanner.com/Hotels/28437/Reservations-West-Lansing-Fairfield-Inn-Lansing-810-Delta-Commerce-Dr-48917.

452. "Causeway Bay Lansing Hotel $104 ($110) - Prices & Reviews – MI." *TripAdvisor*, www.tripadvisor.com/Hotel_Review-g42391-d2605033-Reviews-Causeway_Bay_Lansing_Hotel-Lansing_Ingham_County_Michigan.html.

453, 454. 54A Judicial District 30 Judicial Circuit. *People of the State of Michigan v Stuart Dunnings, III and Steven Dunnings*. Mar. 2016, www.michigan.gov/documents/ag/Stuart_Dunnings-Affidavit_-_54A_-_Dunnings_516941_7.pdf.

455. Hinkley, Justin A. "Troubled Prosecutor Stuart Dunnings Seeks Retirement Benefits." *Detroit Free Press*, Detroit Free Press, 22 June 2016, www.freep.com/story/news/local/michigan/2016/06/22/troubled-prosecutor-stuart-dunnings-seeks-retirement-benefits/86222702/.

456. 54A Judicial District 30 Judicial Circuit. *People of the State of Michigan v Stuart Dunnings, III and Steven Dunnings*. Mar. 2016, www.michigan.gov/documents/ag/Stuart_Dunnings-Affidavit_-_54A_-_Dunnings_516941_7.pdf.

457. Mencarini, Matt. "Schuette: Dunnings Paid for Sex 'Hundreds of Times'." *Lansing State Journal*, Lansing, 14 Mar. 2016, www.lansingstatejournal.com/story/news/local/2016/03/14/ags-office-announce-charges-against-prosecutor-dunnings/81758756/.

458. "The Perceptual Adaptation Experiment of George Stratton and Synaesthesia." *Visual Meditation*, 18 Oct. 2017, visualmeditation.co/the-perceptual-adaptation-experiment-of-george-stratton-and-synaesthesia/.

459-461. Nicolas, Serge & Ferrand, Ludovic. (1999). Wundt's Laboratory at Leipzig in 1891. History of psychology. 2. 194-203. 10.1037//1093-4510.2.3.194.

462. "The Perceptual Adaptation Experiment of George Stratton and Synaesthesia." *Visual Meditation*, 18 Oct. 2017, visualmeditation.co/the-perceptual-adaptation-experiment-of-george-stratton-and-synaesthesia/.

Additional Notes

8. Semantics is the branch of linguistics and logic concerned with meaning. There are a number of branches and sub-branches of semantics, including *formal semantics*, which studies the logical aspects of meaning, such as sense, reference, implication, and logical form, *lexical semantics*, which studies word meanings and word relations, and *conceptual semantics*, which studies the cognitive structure of meaning.

9. *Cognitive structures* are the basic mental processes people use to make sense of information. Other names for cognitive structures include mental structures, mental tools, and patterns of thought.

10. This is referred to as *Lexical Semantics:* The study of word meanings and word relations

A portion of the proceeds from the sale of "27 Seconds" goes to Eve's Angels and The Armed Campaign. For more information, go to:

www.evesangels.org

www.armedcampaign.org